Running Things

The Art of Making Things Happen

Philip B. Crosby

McGraw-Hill Book Company

New York St. Louis San Francisco Auckland Bogotá
Hamburg Johannesburg London Madrid
Mexico Montreal New Delhi Panama
Paris São Paulo Singapore
Sydney Tokyo Toronto

Library of Congress Cataloging-in-Publication Data

Crosby, Philip B.
  Running things.

  Includes index.
  1. Leadership.   2. Management.   I. Title.
HD57.7.C76 1986   658.4'092   85-23743
ISBN 0-07-014513-X

    4567890   **DODO**   89876

ISBN 0-07-014513-X

The editors for this book were William A. Sabin and Jim Bessent,
the designer was Naomi Auerbach, and the production supervisor
was Thomas G. Kowalczyk. It was set in Baskerville by TCSystems.

Printed and bound by R.R. Donnelley and Sons

To Peggy

Running Things

Contents

Preface

THE ART OF BEING THE CHIEF

When I was in Woodsdale grammar school in Wheeling, West Virginia, some time ago—roughly between the use of slate and chalk and the beginning of computers—I began to recognize that some people could lead and others couldn't.

The principal would walk into the room, and in a few moments everyone was involved in something she had suggested. There were no obvious commands or finger pointings—it all seemed sort of spontaneous. We fell in happily and participated. Very few of the teachers could make it happen that way; they needed to rely on authority and that didn't always work.

During my Navy experience, I began to realize that although everyone was superior to me in rank, a few didn't need a title to make something happen. The other side of this was that rank didn't help others; they just somehow couldn't get it all together. Success or failure in this regard didn't seem to be a matter of how much knowledge the individual had on the subject. It was much more personal than that.

My perception on the gift of leadership hasn't changed much since those days. I have worked for several companies and under dozens of people. Many of my bosses were considered to be super-successful. In private life I have served as a church worker in every role possible, short of being the minister. I even played the organ in a couple of clutches. Civic clubs, art support activities, fund drives, little league, and similar community functions have seen me serving as lead and leader. I even chaired the battle against placing a new sewer system in our neighborhood.

We all do these things, they are part of our social structure, and for the most part they are enjoyable. The variety of experience has not changed my observation that some folks can run things and other folks just can't. I used to think that it was something built in, sort of genetic. My conclusion now is that leadership can be learned, provided the individual wants to work at it. Some people are natural leaders, whether they want to be or not. The rest of us have to be more methodical.

The idea for this book came about as a result of something that was said in a hallway conversation after one of our Quality College classes in Winter Park, Florida. We had been talking about causing quality to happen in a company, and one of our executive students nervously remarked that his chairman was not going to like what had to be done. The chairman was noted as a financial whiz with hermitlike tendencies. During the hour I had spent in private conversation with the chairman, I had been greatly impressed by his insight, compassion, and just plain smarts. But that person disappeared when faced with employees and was replaced by a cold, stiff, and intimidating authoritarian.

The thought that he would be able to explain quality to the company personnel was not something that filled either of us with confidence.

However, when it came down to the matter, he responded well and did his part beautifully. In preparation for that, I had had to explain what I saw as the problem and what I thought could be done about it. The chairman put me through many paces until he understood it all thoroughly. He really didn't realize that his regular self was a better runner of things than his formal posture.

It became very clear to me early in life that everything had someone in charge of it. The swimming pool had a lifeguard, the classroom had a teacher, the soda shop had an owner, our house had a mother, the different places I worked had a boss—you get the idea.

This person got to decide what I could and could not do in that particular area. Most times it was to their advantage to make me feel comfortable and accommodated, but nevertheless they ran the place.

In my work over the years, it became more apparent to me that the chief established the tone of the organization, laid out the rules, and drove it along. Some flowered, some withered. Church groups, for instance, where the government and the governed were all volunteers, saw success and failure exist in adjoining meeting rooms.

The Navy provided dramatic evidence that there was something to the effect of the leader. I was on a ship that was an absolute joy. We loved every minute of it, the commodore kept pointing out our performance to the others in the squadron, and I seriously toyed with the thought of a naval career. Then a new captain arrived.

Suddenly everything changed. It became a dismal place to live and work. Nothing was appreciated, nothing was ever right. We were guilty until proven innocent and then suspected of being devious at that. It was a terrible experience.

As the leader of a management consulting firm, I have had the privilege of working closely with the senior management of many firms. They range in size from enormous to smaller than our own company.

The large ones had complex organizations that never held still long enough to document. Many of the small ones had no formal organization. Yet in every case, it was always clear who was supposed to be running things.

As I dealt with these people, I became more and more impressed with the way one single individual set the tone of the operation. I began to take note of it in the organizations I came in contact with: small businesses, professionals, and volunteer groups. It was there every time.

I began to write cases and essays on the subject and finally decided to produce this book. My family was not too thrilled that I would do another one so soon after *Quality Without Tears*—they claim I get fuzzy while I am writing. That is probably true.

Leadership is a fascinating subject; all of human history revolves around it. If it weren't for kings and other national leaders, libraries would be the size of phone booths. What would Shakespeare have written about?

But leadership is a practical tool of everyday life. Each of us leads something, even if it is only taking a reluctant animal for a walk each evening. There is no reason that we should not be effective in our tasks.

This book is not for the leaders of the enormous organizations, for kings, or presidents. For the most part, they do not seek advice on these things. I am trying to reach the regular person who is in charge of something: a store, a church group, a fund raising, a scout troop, an apartment complex, a shopping center, a law office, a family, a park, anything that requires people and an objective.

The characters in the following text are figments of my imagination and represent a composite of my experiences over the years. Just like the case histories we use in the Quality College, they have been created for a learning purpose.

One of the requirements for being a successful leader is making time to sit and read and just learn more about the task. Arranging the world to be able to do this is one of the first tests of childhood. Those who are able to keep learning keep progressing. The story of the grasshopper and the ant is worth remembering.

I have always considered myself a closet grasshopper who recognizes that ants survive and prosper while grasshoppers start over again each year. Being practical, I have donned ants' clothes.

I would like to recognize Debbie Eifert, my assistant, for her help in pulling all this together, and Shirley Silbert, who word-processed it all. How they kept track I will never know.

Bill Sabin, my everlastingly patient and pragmatic editor, has kept me between the rails on three books now. Since he is a successful author as well as an editor, I have no recourse but to be grateful.

PHILIP CROSBY
The Landings
Savannah, Georgia

Running Things

Chapter

1

The Purpose
of an Organization

What is the symphony for?

Why does Jones Ball Bearings Company, Inc., exist?

What does the bank contribute to the community?

How about Scouts? Little League? United Appeal? The National Teachers Association? There are around 58,000 associations in the United States alone, more than 4 million small businesses, untold volunteer organizations, churches by the dozen, and colleges and universities in most counties.

What are all of these for? To make a profit—in the case of companies? To do good? To further some interests? What could they possibly have in common?

It always tickles me when the managers of an organization describe its purpose. They are correct, of course, when they state the obvious contribution that it makes. But they miss the point—that is why most organizations are not as well managed as they could be.

The point is that the purpose of organizations is to help people have lives. Lives come from the challenges and support that people derive from being responsible, being supplied, or being cared for.

How many organizations does a fairly normal person touch or get touched by? There are an incredible number: some we work for, others we belong to, and most of them do something for us.

Everything about us came from some organization: home, mattress, sheets, blankets, robe, electricity, coffee, toilet articles, hair blower, breakfast food, clothes, newspapers, office buildings, restaurants, retail stores, computer, typewriter, books, pens, desks, heating, air-conditioning, sidewalks, lawyers, doctors, dentists, taxis, buses, subways, automobiles, gasoline, groceries, television, radio, theaters, symphonies, luggage, airplanes, hotels, ships—there are several thousand more that serve us in some way.

Then there are the organizations that we actually are part of, the ones we have joined. These contribute much more directly to our lives.

Our employer involves us with several groups that are significant: insurance companies, pension fund, credit union, company social groups, industry associations, and, of course, the organization chart which creates and uncreates relationships.

Then we join others: church (and within the church the choir, the Sunday school, the service committees), PTA, night school, golf club, tennis club, health club, automobile club, bridge group, hospital volunteers, charity drive, bowling team, softball team, garden club, poker club, investment club—to name a few. Each of these offers subdivisions.

After all this, we have to deal with a few more in order to help manage the material aspects of our lives: banks, union, brokerage, life insurance companies, plumbers, garbage collectors, etc.

There are dozens of organizations that affect us, and probably no two people have identical lists. The pleasure and fullness of our lives are very much affected by the way these operations view themselves. If they are managed in one dimension only—to make a profit, say—then they will care little about how we fare in the relationship. We will return the favor and the total group will suffer accordingly, with all parties wondering, perhaps, why no one loves them.

The difference between a well-managed organization and one that just bumps along is multidimensional leadership. Success is the result of usefulness, which in turn comes from an understanding of what is necessary to make things happen.

The useful organization can be constructed and managed in an atmosphere of joy and satisfaction. It is much less work than spending every day feeling as though one were "pushing a safe through the sand." The first part of causing success is to remember that the purpose of an organization is to help people have lives. In a company that believes this, the results are obvious.

"This is such a wonderful place to work. I'd come here for nothing if I had to," said Carol.

"Just what do they do that is so 'wonderful'? It looks to me like you are very busy."

"Busy is not the word. Most of the time I'm swamped. But we all work together and things get done on time. This is a growing firm and we take our work very seriously."

"How about salaries and benefits? Are they comparable with other companies in their field?"

"Yes. In fact, I think they pay a little more. We had a report at the monthly company meeting that said benefits amounted to 35 percent of pay—that's more than most of the big companies pay. And we receive incentive compensation each year that is based on a percentage of pretax profits and our personal contribution to the success of the company."

"All that sounds pretty generous. Does the company make any money?"

"Twelve percent after tax last year, and we had three different outings during the year, including a formal awards dinner. They were a lot of fun."

"And how are you doing personally?"

"Well, my husband and I just bought our first home, the children are happy in their nursery—the company helps pay for that also—and he is taking his master's at night."

"How can the company afford so many benefits and such a

high pay rate and still make 12 percent after tax? That's incredible. Do they have a reason?"

"The president says that the key financial measurement is revenue per employee. If that's high enough, then we can do all the things we want to and still take great care of the stockholders. If you look at other companies in our business, you'll see that they have more employees than we do and their employees don't do as well at the job. We take our work seriously and we make very few errors."

"Is that because you work harder? That sounds like it would wear off eventually."

"Oh, I don't think we work harder than other companies, but we spend a lot of time being trained and we're very careful about establishing procedures. We have a Procedures Committee that we all make inputs to—so the way we work is something we have all agreed upon. That way, we can depend on each other."

"How does everyone know enough about the business? I hear people say things like that, but it seems to me that in the real world there just wouldn't be enough information to go around."

"Well, we just find out what the object of the procedure is supposed to be and work it out. Once you get the hang of it, there is very little problem. We are very professional about it, so there is no squabbling the way there is in some groups I belong to."

"How do you define 'professional'?"

"That's easy. See this block of walnut on my desk? It holds my ballpoint, but it also has engraving on it that says what 'professional' means in this company: ADEPT—Accurate, Discreet, Enthusiastic, Productive, and Thrifty. Everyone gets an ADEPT block from the chairperson the day he or she joins the company. It is a big help."

"If you could give advice to people who were about to take command of some organization, what would you tell them?"

"Treat people the way you would like to be treated; help everyone work hard and achieve results."

"All that is very easy to agree with, but not so easy to do. However, I am glad that everything is going so well with you."

Not all organizations are easy to lead. The leader has to establish the way things are going to go. Sometimes inappropriate procedures become deeply ingrained because no one has taken the initiative. Take the case of the National Society of Picture Hangers . . .

The chairman tapped a spoon against a glass in the classic manner of gaining attention. As the murmur of discussion dropped respectfully, he smiled at the group.

"I am pleased to call the quarterly meeting of the board of directors of the National Society of Picture Hangers to order. The first item of business today is to hear from our new president, Mr. Ellery Wilson.

"Ellery, as you all know, has been a member of the NSPH for 20 years. He is one of our most forward-thinking members. The Nominating Committee asked Ellery to take time from his busy schedule to do this job.

"He agreed to do so only if the board would support his efforts. We assured him of that support. [Applause.]

"This is not a good time for the NSPH. The do-it-yourself fad is still hitting our business. People just pound a tack into the wall and hang pictures anywhere. The professional requirements that our members respect are not considered at all.

"We need to take drastic action or the society and our profession will be as extinct as the dinosaur. Let's hear from our president."

As Ellery stood, the board members greeted him with applause and encouraging comments. The chairman shook his hand and sat back to listen.

"I thank you for that welcome," said Ellery. "These are indeed difficult times. I have been very concerned for some time that our profession was in danger. Hanging pictures has been my life, and I want to make certain that my children have the opportunity to be NSPH members as well.

"I see three problems that we have to overcome. I would like to list them for you and then offer my recommendations for action. We have very little time."

A member raised his hand. "I hate to interrupt you, Ellery, but I need to ask the chairman something. Shouldn't we have had the approval of the minutes of the last meeting before getting on to new business?"

The chairman glared at him. "I suppose so, but I felt that it was more important for us to get right into this survival program."

"The rules of order are very clear, and it is not proper for us to ignore them," replied the member.

"As long as we have started this way, we will continue" said the chairman. "We will catch up at the end of the meeting."

"I must protest" said another member. "If we don't follow our own agenda, we can never expect to get anything done."

"There will be time enough later," snarled the chairman. "Let's let Ellery get on with his comments."

Ellery nodded and then found his place again.

"As I said, there are three areas in which we need to take action. First, we are not known to the public. Decorators and architects know about us, but not the public. I feel that we are going to need to advertise. I took the liberty of talking informally with two agencies, and they both feel we can have a very effective program at a relatively low cost."

Another member raised his hand.

"No commitments can be made without the approval of the Finance Committee. We have no budget for advertising."

"Advertising is unprofessional anyhow," said another. "Doctors and lawyers don't advertise, and they get along all right."

"They are starting to do it."

"Well, it just isn't professional. My customers wouldn't understand if I was on TV every night talking about how they shouldn't bang tacks into the wall."

"The program I am suggesting would be very discreet," said Ellery. "It would be primarily in home buyers' magazines and grocery store newspapers. We haven't talked money because I knew I would need approval. But perhaps we can do that today."

"As chairman of the Finance Committee, I would be glad to expedite the request. We will have our next meeting in 3 months. Perhaps you could send us a proposal to review by that time. We can recommend something for next year's budget."

Ellery stared. "We can talk about it after the meeting. Let me get on to the second item. This concerns our homeowners' qualification system. By asking homeowners to fill out a six-page form before we hang their pictures, we may be providing a source of irritation. I am going to recommend that we discontinue that form."

There was a moment of stunned silence.

"That form was developed after careful study. We wanted to make certain that the customers were able to pay and that there were enough pictures to be hung to make it worthwhile. It is an important thing, and you can't just throw it out because you think it is an irritant."

Another member stood up. "That is why we have a board, to protect the members from wild ideas. The next thing you'll want to do is change the name of the society."

Ellery blushed. "Actually, that is the next item on my list. Our members are getting into hanging many different items in houses. To limit our name to picture hanging is a problem."

"But we have had this name for 40 years. It has served us well."

"I had only planned to mention it at this time," said Ellery. "My thought was that we could appoint a team to consider the alternatives and make a recommendation to the board."

The executive secretary motioned for attention. "The bylaws require a vote of the membership in order to change the name of the society. There would have to be two-thirds of the total membership in favor. We have never had a two-thirds vote on anything. Changing the name would be impossible."

"Mr. Chairman, I move that we go back to the agenda and cover the minutes of the last meeting."

"Second the motion."

"Call the question."

The chairman looked at Ellery and shrugged in resignation.

"All in favor?" he asked.

"Aye," shouted the group.

"Opposed?" he asked.

"No," said three members.

"The 'ayes' have it. We will return to the beginning of the agenda. The president will make his remarks later."

"Not likely," said the president. "I think I will go home and find some other way to expand my business."

The mistake Ellery made was that he thought the board of directors was interested in improving the picture-hanging business. Actually the board members were interested in having authority over the society.

Beginning an executive assignment with incorrect assumptions is a guaranteed system for failing.

People band together to accomplish something; that is why we have families, nations, companies, and such. Often the purpose of that banding is forgotten after the basic needs are achieved. Yet the organization stays intact to work on something else—if the purpose is redescribed to the members.

"Giving people lives" refers to a great many characteristics. Lives are the result of education, support, work, and relationships. In the same way that children are raised in a family so that they will grow up with the information and skills needed to begin their own families, people are raised in formal organizations.

Leadership provides the definitions and opportunities for the members. If it does not do that, the members get off on the wrong track and the organization becomes inoperative.

Chapter

2

The Role of the Leader

There has been a great deal written about leadership over the years. This book is not an attempt to reverse all of that. Every organization needs a leader and usually has one. More often than not, the organization's success or lack of it is directly due to the effectiveness of the leader.

The leader causes the creation of the lifestyle of the organization. This can happen through direct positive action or indirect negative action. Doing nothing also creates a lifestyle.

Sometimes people don't need a leader at all. In the 1985 Mexico City earthquake, for example, individuals just moved right into the task of digging people out of the rubble and providing for the basics of life. The government acted as quickly as possible, but a lot had already been accomplished by the time activities were organized.

I know of no failproof script on leadership success. But I do know of a few things that have to happen. In establishing the lifestyles that produce a successful operation, things have to be *arranged, established, exampled, handled,* and *done.*

The most difficult management jobs are those in which assumptions are made about the participation of the people involved. Ellery assumed that the members of the NSPH were dedicated to the same results he envisioned. They weren't. Many a general has been led astray by the impression that all soldiers are interested in fighting on command.

Mothers and fathers are astonished in each generation to learn that their offspring have different ideas about what is important.

In a business situation, the leader is more careful. Ellery would have worked to get a charter established; then he would have laid out the purpose and the implementation process, using the necessary steps of leadership. He would have make certain that the members felt they were part of it all, and he would have insisted on some measurements that would lay the groundwork for appreciation.

The commonsense things he wanted to do were completely ignored by the board members because they had another agenda entirely. What they wanted to do was follow the rules of order, go to meetings, control something, and receive awards. He had a hard time believing it.

The fault was his, clearly. He broke his own rules of management because he assumed that everyone wanted to accomplish something worthwhile. He felt that he could just hit the ground running and get things done. He should have known better.

There are basic actions that have to be taken in order to make any management job successful. The organization makes little difference. Families are much harder to run than big companies; church groups, Scouts, and fund-raisers all have their degrees of difficulty.

I have had all levels of jobs in business, from junior technician to chief executive. The main difference is that mistakes get more expensive as you go along. Some of those mistakes are the result of misjudgment, but the majority come about because something is taken for granted.

Companies regularly introduce new products that no one buys. Stores open with great hope and close when they are not accepted. Housing developments perish alongside those that prosper. Individuals triumph in one situation and despair in another. Success often breeds failure.

The common entity in all operations, successful or not, is the leader. Someone has to run everything, and that someone has the most influence over whether an effort will be successful. Leadership is not a scientific subject; a great deal depends on components that are not entirely clear.

Take colleges, for instance. Although most of them teach management, they practice very little of it. For the most part, they fumble along, usually one step ahead of financial disaster. Yet they do survive.

Very few businesses exist today that have been around as long as the "inefficient" colleges from which they obtain their employees. Yet businesses work very hard at managing, while colleges work hard at teaching and being. This could be a source of wonder. Is all of management's scrambling around necessary?

Actually, organizations such as colleges, churches, and art galleries exist and grow because people want them to. Very few people care whether the Smith Mattress Company lives or dies, except, of course, the Smiths and their dealers.

When I speak of the church, I don't mean The Church. I am talking about the members of the neighborhood congregation and the buildings they use. How does a small group of people keep their organization up and going all those years? What do they know that the big companies don't know?

During the course of this book I will discuss several aspects of running things, including the witness of the leader and the evaluation of the led. But before that, I need to build a structure that applies to any situation. This is not an attempt to provide a system of leadership that always succeeds. I doubt that such a process could ever exist. If it did, all the fun would go out of the subject.

The structure relates to the vessel that is being guided, much like a ship or plane. It is of little use having controls to waggle if they are not attached to anything. The titles and visible signs that go along with power do not produce power all by themselves. The way the leader uses them to cause action determines their worth.

I once worked for a company that acquired many businesses. The managers of a purchased company were treated well and were expected to continue running everything. Usually their salaries were increased to be in line with similar jobs in the parent company. Additional capital was made available along with expert counseling in many areas. The result, in most cases, was improved productivity, a larger market share, and success in general.

One fallout in the whole arrangement was that a new chief executive was usually appointed. The old one was promoted to chairperson of the board and given vague corporate assignments. This effectively eliminated any lingering control over the company and permitted the new owners to take actions necessary for improvement. So this person sitting in the same office, with the same perks and worth a lot more money than before, actually had little to say about what was going on.

There are also cases in which the executive has all the right authority but can make little happen. This was what Ellery went through with the NSPH experience. Enough people have to cooperate if the organization is going to run. There is a minimum mass that must be assembled. Getting people to cooperate enthusiastically—well, that is what leadership is all about.

3

Arranging

The key to cooperation is having all the people know what it is they are cooperating about. This requires some specifics, such as *charter, purpose, requirements, dedication,* and *attitude.*

CHARTER

Symphony Drive

We will establish a permanent symphony orchestra staffed by professional musicians that will perform two seasons each year. The symphony will be funded 60 percent by subscription and performance and 40 percent by solicited donations from citizens and corporate sponsors. The symphony will be professionally managed and overseen by a board of directors chosen from sponsors.

Neighborhood Cleanup

We will establish a cleanup committee in our neighborhood that will pick up the casual trash that finds its way to our streets and vacant lots. This volunteer organization will be set up so that everyone may participate and no one will have a burden.

New Product

We will create, develop, and market a portable hair dryer that will weigh less than 2 pounds, fit in a carry-on travel bag, have its own identifiable package, sell for under $10, meet our gross margins, and be attractive.

With these charters, the involved individuals can become a team by having a common understanding of the planned result of the effort. A charter needs to be measurable:

- Permanent symphony orchestra
  - Professional musicians
  - Funded 60 percent by subscriptions, 40 percent by donations
  - Professionally managed
- Neighborhood cleanup committee
  - Casual trash
  - Volunteer organization
- Portable hair dryer
  - Weigh less than 2 pounds
  - Fit in a travel bag
  - Have identifiable package
  - Sell for under $10
  - Meet gross margins
  - Be attractive

Each of these characteristics can be reviewed and displayed on a chart and can serve as the basis for the regular status review meetings that all successful projects require.

We can watch the struggle the development people have with finding a motor that not only will be powerful enough to drive the hair dryer but will not add so much weight that the 2-pound limit will be threatened.

We can see how many volunteers can be found without blackmail to join the trash pickup detail.

We can track the group that is identifying and auditioning professional musicians and determine how many offers will need to be made and how many musicians will need to be brought in from out of town. We can participate as the determination of ticket prices is made and auditorium fees are negotiated.

With a clear charter, the group has a chance at success. The first meeting should be dedicated to writing the charter and agreeing on its distribution.

PURPOSE

Symphony Drive

The symphony will provide live music for our citizens who now have to travel up to 300 miles to hear it; it will give children a basis for understanding fine music; and it will upgrade the city in the minds of companies seeking to locate their businesses in a progressive community.

Neighborhood Cleanup

Through-traffic, both pedestrian and vehicular, in our neighborhood is a source of discarded paper, cans, and other trash. Also, some residents have been dumping leaves and cuttings in vacant lots. The city cannot be expected to deal with such casual debris. By keeping our neighborhood clean, we will discourage further littering. We have to do it ourselves.

New Product

Several of our products reach the traveling person, but market surveys show that we are viewed as being limited to creams and cosmetics. The hair dryer will give us an entrée to more active products and broaden our image. If accepted, it will be the beginning of a whole new market penetration.

So the charter sets "it" up and the purpose describes why we want to do "it." People *do* need a reason for doing. Many organizations assume that people will just do whatever is assigned. It appears that they do, but in reality they just go through the motions. They never really put themselves into the job until they understand what their personal roles are in making the project happen.

All individuals want to make a contribution. They just have to know what is expected of them. I envy the high school football players of today, for instance. They can watch the professionals play ball on television. Experts describe each play, and slow-motion videos show the great players making the moves that produce results.

With this type of information, the young players can learn more about what to do. When I was their age, it was hard to find much helpful material. We learned from watching each other, with predictable results.

What I never really understood was the requirements. What exactly was I supposed to do? The coaches tried very hard, but they knew so much about it and we knew so little that communication was difficult. It is the same with golf. Every year I find out something that others have known for years.

If employees are being asked to "do it right the first time," then they are entitled to know what "it" is. Once the "it" is understood, it is possible to determine what tools are required and what assistance might be needed.

The "it" consists of the requirements.

REQUIREMENTS

Symphony Drive

- Establish organizational format.
- Determine personnel requirements for symphony.
- Determine material requirements for symphony.
- Set up and conduct subscription system.
- Set up and conduct donation and foundation drive.
- Select professional manager.

- Select musicians.
- Obtain concert hall.
- Determine and publish performance schedule.

All these tasks need to be accomplished, although not necessarily in the order listed above. Each one lends itself to a committee or staff assignment. The first thing to do is to work out the details for accomplishment and decide who is going to do each task. Everyone will know what his or her role is, and management can keep track of the progress.

Requirements are communications—that is all. Some aspects of a job will never have anything done about them unless they are spelled out. Requirements must be taken seriously or they don't matter.

DEDICATION

When dedication to the task becomes the subject of discussion, it must be said that all projects fold together. The leader has no more important concern than helping all the people involved reach the conclusion that they are important to the undertaking and it is important to their world.

This cannot be taken for granted. When the space program started some time ago, I thought that it would be easy to keep people interested in quality. After all, a person's life was at stake. However, I soon realized that this awareness quickly disappeared when left to itself. Everyone needed to be reminded continually. And when you think of it, is there any product that can't do harm to people if it is defective?

Dedication cannot be considered a given. It has to be arranged, nurtured, pruned, and cultured. Everyone has to find a personal reason for doing the task.

I used to hear management snarl: "They get paid for the job. If they do it well, they get to keep it." This was the motivation approach of the past. There are some folks who work for money alone, but they are loyal only to money. They will leave you for a small raise across the street. Everyone I ever knew who was dedicated to making a lot of dough never did. Those who had a cause or an idea that they had to see succeed were the ones who made out. And they usually were surprised at the result.

People work for fulfillment, appreciation, and companionship. This applies to volunteers and professionals alike. Employees need to receive money from their jobs; that is part of having a life. But it isn't the most important part of a job. It probably isn't even in the top five.

If people are going to be dedicated to a task, then the task has to be worthy of them and they need to feel that they are special. "This worthy task won't get done unless these worthy people perform it." And that has to be the truth. Being phony will never help dedication emerge.

Dedication comes from understanding the job and from being able to feel the results of personal effort. A symphony organization requires a large amount of hands-on activity, from planning the events to seating the customers. It is very easy to lose one's identity.

People will apply for and accept paying jobs that do not necessarily turn them on. They feel dedication will come later. It is like marrying a friend and hoping love will emerge. Sometimes it does, but usually it doesn't.

Volunteer organizations have the advantage that very few people join without being interested in the work—or at least in the status that such work brings.

Before people come to an organization, they have their own ideas about what happens inside it. It is absolutely vital to give them a complete orientation as soon as they arrive so that they will know what really goes on and what their role is to be. The orientation has to begin on the first day and should be done in a planned and dignified manner. It is similar to boot camp, where my comrades and I learned to be sailors. That took several weeks of concentrated attention and the understanding that there was no way out. We all learned.

New employees or volunteers should be greeted as though they were guests and immediately shown a film or slide show about the history of the organization. The *charter* and *purpose* have to be made clear—and should be included in the procedures manual given to each newcomer.

Tours of the facilities and meetings with the individuals who run things are an important part of the orientation. Then new employees should be placed with their immediate supervisor, who explains the business of requirements. Here they learn that their position is key to helping others do their jobs. At this time, the specific training they will receive is explained. They will be taught to meet their requirements.

As they absorb all this information, the newcomers will want to hear about the future and their personal opportunity to grow with it. They will want something to take back with them to show the family. And they need an assignment, work to do right away. Real work.

Dedication is initially aimed at the organization itself and will continue that way if everything has been represented accurately. It is not advisable to paint a picture of competence and affluence during the orientation if that is not the real world. Tell them the truth, and let them help fix it. Everyone wants to be needed.

ATTITUDE

So much has been written and said about positive attitudes that we might all be expected to possess them. Actually, I think most people are positive, at least until their world teaches them the futility of such an approach.

Most leadership is negative in that it is directed at not failing. Not failing is not the same as succeeding. It implies a cautious sort of fallback approach. What we want to do is have all individuals feel comfortable about themselves and the organization. We want them to be positive—it is more rewarding and more fun.

Organizations have an attitude that is generated by the thought leaders. Normally, these are titular leaders, but that is not always so. Sometimes there are people in operations who influence attitudes in ways that the leadership does not recognize. The personnel department can easily become a negative force by harassing everyone. Any department can, as well as people who have been around for some time and keep stating that nothing will ever change.

The leader must make certain that attitudes are correct by conducting a continuing and well-organized process of example and teaching. It all begins with the performance requirements of the entity.

All employees want to be proud of everything they are connected with and, if given the slightest opportunity, will make it something of which to be proud. Management just has to be the catalyst.

During my career in quality management, the most difficult obstacle was the generally accepted conviction that everything just couldn't get done right the first time. It was the ultimate in self-fulfilling prophecies. After all, the evidence was everywhere. Since the belief was so deeply ingrained, little effort was made to do what was necessary to get things done correctly. The whole practice of quality control, for instance, is based on the statistical process which contains no zero.

Manufacturing operations, in particular, would install programs to improve quality and would be disappointed when very little happened. White-collar areas entered into such activities only at the lowest possible levels.

Nothing really began to change until managers finally were taught to think about the process of "unquality." Once they realized how much "unquality" cost—25 percent of sales in manufacturing, 45 percent of operating costs in administrative or service companies—they began to take quality seriously.

As soon as the leadership began to be serious about quality and to place it at the top of the significance list, everyone else got involved. Dramatic improvement began to take place, not because of some program, but because attention was being paid.

Companies put out quality policies that said, "We will deliver defect-free products and services to our customers on time." However, they made it clear that the customer may not be the user of the final service or product. The customer was the person who used the work, perhaps the person at the next desk.

Volunteer organizations began to pick up this concept and apply it to their work. I know of a church staff whose members quit blaming everything on each other and worked out a clear list of requirements about who was going to do what. All the managers of the "art" operations (symphony, ballet, gallery, etc.) came to a special class and were amazed to find out that they had the same problems as billion-dollar corporations.

The performance-standard question has become confused over the years. It had been thought, and taught, that the standard of how much quality was required varied with the job. We now know that people really prefer a consistent standard, the same one all the time.

Each operation has to have a standard that cannot be misunderstood. "Defect-free" or "zero defects" is a way of saying, "Perform exactly like the requirement." "Do it right the first time" is another way of saying the same thing. The main thing is not to have any waffle or wiggle, no "That's close enough."

When the people in charge and the ones doing the work all take requirements seriously, then things get done right. No program or supernumerary influence will affect that.

To convince everyone that they are serious, managers have to continually witness and teach.

When I worked at Bendix in the 1950s as a reliability engineer, I did not make enough money to support my family, so I also worked in a men's clothing store on the weekends and a couple of nights a week. This was Gilbert's in South Bend.

I had sold shoes all the time I went to college, women's shoes, at a big store in Cleveland. I was a pretty good shoe salesman, but it was all intuitive because no one ever showed me anything about selling shoes. Gilbert's sold men's clothes and had a full line of very fine merchandise. The store had a good range: Hart, Shaffner, and Marks suits, GGG suits, Florsheim shoes, Allen Edmunds, and everything else a man would ever want in clothes. Gilbert's had a good credit policy too.

Mr. Stanley Gilbert stood at the front door and greeted everybody coming in, and Mr. Marcus Gilbert stood back by the cash register and ran the business. When they hired me as a part-time shoe salesman, they brought the Florsheim traveling representative in to show me about shoes. This man came with a box full of shoes that broke apart.

He showed me how shoes are made, and he showed me how to fit shoes. I'll bet there aren't four people I know whose shoes fit. Nobody knows how to fit shoes anymore. It's one of those lost arts. He spent all afternoon with me. Then Mr. Gilbert and the floorwalker spent time with me, explaining the pricing system.

When half the shoes in a particular lot were sold, they marked the remaining pairs down to half price. If a customer came in and wanted size 10½C shoes, I could sell him the pair he wanted and then tell him, "I've got another pair over here at half price that will fit you too"; I often sold both pairs. Then they set it up so that I was paid 50 cents for each pair of shoes I sold. But if I sold double, that was an additional 50 cents. So the difference for me between one pair of shoes and two was $1.

Around the middle of the month they would have a meeting, with a deli buffet and some camaraderie. Somebody, such as the Arrow Shirt salesperson, would come and tell us about shirts, how they were made, and how to fit a shirt.

They schooled us on what to do with a person who finished buying shoes. We learned to say, "What else are you interested in today?" If the reply was, "I need a new sport jacket," then we would take the customer over to the sport jackets. They showed us how to fit jackets. If we had trouble, we would get one of the sport-jacket salespeople to assist the customer.

I understood what I was doing. I used to make more money at Gilbert's than I made at my regular job, which wasn't too hard. The Gilberts set requirements very clearly, gave me the tools and the information to do the job, and then helped me. One day I was standing by the tie counter and a customer came from the cashier with a suit box under his arm. He stopped and looked down at the ties. So I said, "May I help you?" He said, "No, thank you," and went out the door.

Mr. Gilbert came up and said, "Now, Phil, let me show you how to do that. When a man looks at the ties, you say to him, 'That would go very nicely with a gray suit.' He'll say, 'Oh,' and you help him get his box open so that the tie can be laid on the suit. Then fix him up with two or three ties because he needs new ties to go with his suit. You get 10 cents or 20 cents, depending on the tie." So I said, "Mr. Gilbert, how do I know what color suit is in the box?" He said, "Look at the cashier, and the cashier will raise his fingers: one for blue, two for brown, and three for gray."

That's what it is all about. The future executive can go all the way through undergraduate business school and graduate business school without receiving a course on how to help the employee. It's always "systems and programs and analysis," not how do we help the person do the job, how do we help people.

What keeps people from doing their jobs right? It is the proper role of managers to go around and ask, "How are things going? Is there anything I can do to help? What is keeping you from getting any better?" When you start to ask, they will let you know.

The role of the senior manager is to *witness*. People are always looking at top management. Our company went through a recession back in 1982. The whole world did, but I didn't care about the rest of the world. We went through it, and it hurt. Things were very tough, very difficult, and it was touch-and-go as to whether we were going to make it. As I would go around the company, I could see people were observing me. So I went around smiling and offering encouragement. Had I looked perpetually digusted, that could have been the end of it. With such an example, any employee with sense would start seeking another job. The way a leader goes about the job is very much a projection; and when I say leader, I am not talking about just the chairman of the board. You are the leader of what you run.

THE PYGGS

Sometimes, the future can be foretold by the past. A good example is the case of the Pygg family.

Little Jymmie Pygg bounced onto his grandfather's lap. "Tell us the story about when you were young, Papa." "Oh please, please, please, Papa," said his two little brothers.

"You boys know that tale as well as I do," smiled the old man. "You could probably tell it better too."

The boys all huddled around him, so he laid down his book and drew them all onto the couch with him. They gazed up with expectant faces.

"Once upon a time there were three of us boys. Our daddy called us together to tell us that it was time for us to go out in the world and make our fortunes."

"What's a fortune, Papa?"

"Well, it means money, I guess, but our dad was telling us to be successful. He had always told us that we should go build something worthwhile. Then we could live a good life and have children too."

"Like our mommy and daddy?"

"Right. Now let me get this story told, or we'll be late for lunch and be in trouble." The boys settled down.

"Once upon a time there were three of us boys. Our father called us together and said that we should go out into the world and make our fortunes. So we all packed up and got ready to leave.

" 'Before you go, boys,' said our daddy, 'you must always be on the lookout for the Wolves. They make their living by buying up businesses and property that have failed. If you don't do things properly, the Wolves will soon be at your door and it won't be long before they're in and you're out.'

" 'Are they going to attack us, daddy?' I asked. I was afraid.

" 'Oh no, they don't have to do that. They just wait until people fail on their own. Then they pick up the pieces and make something out of them. They get things so cheap, sometimes for nothing, that they don't have to be mean.'

" 'But I thought Wolves were mean and treacherous.'

" 'Perhaps they were back in the old days, but that was when they used to have to hunt for business. Now they have all they can do to handle organizations that fall into their laps.'

"Well, all of us boys put down our bags and stood around our daddy. This didn't sound good at all.

" 'What makes organizations fail, daddy? How can we keep that from happening to us? We don't want to wind up in Mr. Wolf's sack. What will happen to us?'

"He looked pleased. 'I have been waiting for you to ask me,' he said. 'You boys will have to be careful out there because you may not get a second chance. Now let's talk about how you plan to build your houses. Harold, what are your plans?'

"Harold, stood up, brushed the wrinkles out of his pants, and cleared his throat.

" 'I don't want to spend any more money than I have to, so I'm going to make my house out of straw. There is plenty of it lying around. I won't need electricity or heat, so that will save me a lot of money. I'll use these old candles I have been saving for 2 years.'

"Our daddy shook his head. 'All you think about is money, Harold. That is one-dimensional. If you make every decision based only on what it costs, you will never have any structure. When the Wolves come around and ask you how everything is going, their breath will be enough to knock your house down. How about you, Elmer?'

" 'Well, I know that my house has to be solid enough to live in, so I am going to build it out of sticks. But I want to get on with my work and I plan to build it in 1 day so I don't waste any time. That way it won't cost me very much, and it won't take time from important things.'

" 'You will spend more time patching and fixing than you will save,' said daddy. 'And the Wolves might have to ask you two questions before their breath blows down the house. You are as foolish as your brother.'

" 'I am going to build my house out of bricks,' I said, and my daddy nodded in approval.

" 'The way I look at it, I can mix up clay and straw and make bricks without a great deal of expense and then follow a plan so that I use just the right amout of time. It will be a good solid house. The Wolves won't be able to talk it down. Then I will have a solid base to run my organization.'

" 'You will attract good people to work with you if you have a good solid foundation like a brick house.'

" 'But it will cost more money,' said Harold.

" 'And it will take time,' said Elmer.

" 'But it will let him survive when you two are rooting around in the open market looking for something to eat and a place to stay.

" 'There are three dimensions to running something: time, money, and completeness. They have to balance each other, but if something isn't complete, it might as well not have been started.

" 'Do you think one of the Swine girls would be willing to come live in a straw house, heated by a candle? Do you think that the banks will loan anything to someone who has a house made of sticks and has to patch it every night? You boys have to look at the whole picture. Now go out in the world and make your fortunes.' "

"What happened then, Papa?" said the grandchildren.

"Well, everyone did just what they said they were going to do, and sure enough, it all happened just like our daddy said it would. My two brothers are both working for the Wolves' organization for peanuts. They just were never leaders because they only looked at things in a limited way."

"Is that why we all have brick houses?" asked the grandchildren.

"Our family is the leading company in selling bricks to homebuilders. When you grow up, you will have the business to run."

"Bricks are too heavy for me, Papa. I will work with straw," said Harold.

"The Wolves will be glad to hear that."

Chapter

4

Establishing

When I joined the Navy, there was no doubt in my mind that I belonged to an organization. It had uniforms, facilities, rules, regulations, weapons, ships, airplanes, and just about everything else that could be had. It also had a clear organization chart which we all wore on our sleeves.

In boot camp, I soon learned who was in charge and who was supposed to do what. After 40 years I can still remember how to do close-order drill and roll a pair of dungarees into a prescribed package. Admittedly, I don't get much call for either of these skills, but they have a way of hanging on.

As a 17-year-old recruit, in company with 119 others, I was supposed to learn how to exist in the Navy. When I graduated after 6 weeks, I had been trained on how not to embarrass the Navy when I talked, walked, or dressed up in some of the dozens of garments in my duffle bag. Many of my barracks mates had been raised in less fortunate circumstances than I and were thrilled with the thought of owning all those clothes. Things were different back in the 1940s.

In boot camp, we were tested and examined to determine what we were good for. I was assigned to the Hospital Corps

School in San Diego. There they taught me how to be a medical person. When I left HCS, I spent some time in a hospital and then went to the Pacific.

For the next 2 years, I held sick call almost every day, assisted in surgery (with my gloved hands in people's bellies), and got along very well. No one ever got worse because of what I did to them, and, in fact, I helped out a lot of folks.

When I was recalled for the Korean war, I was assigned to the Marine Corps. There I was the medical department for a large group that lived in the woods most of the time. I was sent to Field Medical Service School, which is a kind of Marine boot camp with special teaching.

If something had happened to me at any time during this experience, my seniors would have just called for a replacement. Another third-class hospitalperson would have appeared with the identical skill and dedication I possessed. The system worked.

When it comes to establishing an organization, the leader has to make certain that this type of approach is taken. Obviously, the Navy, because of its size, is more depersonalized than the type of organization I am addressing here. Yet it has survived all these years, even when it fell on hard times financially. It has always been able to do what the nation demanded.

This success has been due to people rather than equipment, but people do need the proper equipment, just as they need an organizational framework, a clear purpose, and all the rest. Most of all, they need to know they belong to something.

Belonging to something is what people center on throughout their lives. There have been so many books and poems written about the desire to belong that one might think we would take it to heart. Yet organizations miss the chance to be spectacular by limiting the dimensions within which they operate.

I have never met an executive who didn't claim to be people-oriented. To me this implies that people come first. However, in real life, they are not what comes first in an organization—at least not naturally. Everyone needs people in order to have success, and that success is a function of the way those people produce.

The framework of an organization is really its identity. How do we know it exists? By the sign in the window? By the trash in the dumpster? By the letterhead on the stationery? It makes you wonder. We tend to take existence for granted.

For the employee, the organization exists when the president says it exists. Bill Clem, the man who made baseball umpires into a professionally respected group, was once asked about the different kinds of pitches and what they were. "They are nothing until I call them something," he replied. The pitch doesn't exist until the umpire says it exists.

The legalities of forming an organization are of interest only to lawyers and other professionals who keep track of such things. No one ever sees the corporation papers again after they are signed.

I have belonged to many groups in my lifetime, from the Boy Scouts to the Interlachen Country Club. The club has visible facilities; the Boy Scouts met in the back room of the church. The club has paid employees; the Scouts were all voluntary. Both aimed at providing some useful activities, but the Scouts gave me a philosophical basis for life. We are supposed to be equipped with that basis before joining a country club.

Most companies expect that their employees will be fully operational at the time they join. They will have the personal drive, composure, skills, and communication ability to make a contribution to the company. In the same way that we learn how to get along in a club—to make friends and use the facilities—we are expected to learn to get along in our new company. The Navy and the Boy Scouts know better.

The head of an organization would not dream of purchasing a new piece of equipment without making certain it fit, would do the job, and could be upgraded if necessary. But the same consideration usually is not given to people. Some things have to be established.

1. Orientation—What are we all about?
2. Systems—What do we do around here?
3. Communication—How do we know what is what?
4. Development—How do we get better?
5. Appreciation—How am I doing?

For example, homeowner associations, those found in real estate developments or condos, exist to make rules to help the members have fuller, happier, more secure lives. Don't they? Well, don't they? A visit to an executive committee meeting will help to make the point.

THE EXECUTIVE COMMITTEE MEETING

Security was obviously concerned as he raised his hand for permission to speak.

"Car decals are a big problem. Some of the residents are being very difficult about filling out the forms and attaching the stickers."

"Don't they want security?" asked the chairperson. "How do they expect us to know who's inside the area if they don't let us tag the cars?"

"They want security. That's one of the reasons they bought here. The complaints we are getting are on the procedure. The request for three pages of information, a copy of the car registration, and the insurance verification seems to upset many of the residents. Those who are ex-military don't mind as much; they are used to it."

"What do they want?"

"Most of them think that owning a house here is enough verification and that we should just put a sticker on any car they own."

"That would be ridiculous. Who knows what might happen to those stickers? What about the transient traffic and the building subcontractors?"

"They get a pass from the guard each day, except for the ones who are in here all the time. We give *them* a sticker. It's easy to identify a vehicle when it's a big truck with lettering on the side."

"How about insurance for them?"

"We assume they have it. They wouldn't be very good business people if they didn't."

"Well, the residents will just have to go along with the plan.

If any of them complain too much, we'll just make them leave their cars outside the gate and walk in. That will send everyone a message."

"What is the status of the golf course operations?"

Golf rearranged her papers.

"Basically, everything is moving along smoothly. There are three areas in which we are having difficulties. Tee times are always a problem. We only take reservations the day before, and some of the residents complain that we should do it 2 days before so that they can plan better."

"That would mean a lot more bookkeeping," said the chairperson. "We don't have enough help as it is."

"Then we've been getting complaints about the pro shop closing at 4:00 P.M. and carts having to be in by that time. I've told the members that this lets us keep the staff small, but they still get upset every day. Many of them would like to buy their own carts."

"These people are just going to have to learn that we are running this association with their best interests in mind. If they want us to meet the budget, then they are going to have to cooperate. What is your last problem?"

"We have a sign that says 'No golf shoes in the lounge.' "

"It's been there for years. What could possibly be wrong with that? No one wants spikes to tear up the carpet."

"Well, many of these new golf shoes don't have spikes. They are more like tennis shoes than golf shoes. They work well on the course, and they don't make any impression on the carpet. When we tell the members they can't wear those shoes inside, they get very upset with us."

"That's a clear case of people trying to bend the rules because of a technicality. If we change the sign to say 'No spikes in the lounge,' it will look like we don't know what we're doing. The residents will lose confidence in our leadership. There will probably be jokes about it. No, we will stick by our guns, and if any residents make a big deal about it, we will take them before the board and suspend them for 30 days. Any more items?"

Accounting nodded for recognition.

"I have one rather sticky item. This refers to the interest

charges on club and association bills. Almost everyone pays within 30 days, and once in a while someone goes out to 60 days. Usually that's because they're off on vacation or traveling or something.

"Since the beginning of the year, we have been charging interest on accounts after the first week. Many of the members have been paying the original amount and have not been including the interest. They say that they're not going to pay it and that charging interest is illegal. The attorneys say that it is not illegal and that we have every right to charge it."

"How much money are we talking about?" asked the chairperson.

"At present, the delinquencies total $6,359.12. That doesn't include this week's postings."

"How many members are involved?"

"About thirty."

"You say the attorneys feel we are on solid ground?"

"No question about that."

"Then we have to make it clear that we are serious. Put a note in the next bill that any accounts with delinquent interest will be turned over to a credit agency for collection. That will get the message across."

Golf nodded. "It sure is a pleasure to work with you. You go right to the heart of the matter and take the action necessary. At the last two clubs where I worked, the committee coddled the members and gave them everything they wanted. It made my job very hard."

The chairperson smiled. "Leadership is not as hard as people make out. The most important thing is to set policy and then never ever change from it. That way the staff members know they have something that can be relied on.

"And the customers—in this case, the members—have to know that a firm hand is on the tiller. If they think they can just do whatever they want, well, the result is chaos."

Comment: Management on a daily basis is made up of finding solutions for problems. Some of these problems are the result of twigs that were bent dozens of years ago; some were invented this very moment.

The way an organization analyzes and attacks its problems says a great deal about it. One of the best evaluation characteristics refers to "who is at fault." Sometimes it is not all that clear, as is evident in the following situation.

MINUTES OF ANNUAL MEETING OF THE INTERNATIONAL
TOURIST PRODUCTIVITY BOARD, BRIGHTON, ENGLAND

The chairperson called the meeting to order and the previous minutes were approved. Because of the urgency of the subject, the chairperson directed that the meeting would proceed immediately to the report by the Special Committee on Tourist Problems. Lord Faltmorthe reported:

Studies show that individual tourists are just not performing as well as in the past. It is regretful, but they are falling down on the job. We have listed several specifics and commend them to you for your consideration.

Frankly, we are at a loss to explain the behavior pattern we see developing. It is as though tourists think productivity is not very important. We can use your input. If you have any ideas for reversing this trend, please let me or any member of the committee know. Here are the items:

- The TPT (time per tourist) in castle visiting has dropped from 4.3 hours in 1976 to 2.6 hours in 1984. This has devastated the guide forces. Their morale has crumbled as tourists insist on faster discourses so that they can move out into the air again.
- Bus movement without a bathroom stop has dropped from 3.75 hours to 2.16 hours. I don't need to tell you what this frequent delay pattern does to schedules.
- Tourists are leaving the hotel on their free days an average of 45 minutes later for local sightseeing and returning 35 minutes earlier than in the past. That gives the community over 1 hour a day less time to assist tourists.
- One of the most insidious trends has been reported just recently. Tourists are having leisurely and relaxed lunches at restaurants. The efficient lunchrooms supplied by museums and castles are being neglected. They may have to raise their prices.
- The purchase of useless trinkets is deteriorating.
- Several tour groups have reported that some tourists refused to leave all their luggage in the lobby before going to bed. They claimed that this made getting dressed and bathed in the morning difficult.

What all this means is that our essential measurement of four attractions per day is just not being met. We would actually prefer six, but that is out of the question unless we can improve the individual tourist productivity rate.

We must face up to the fact that tourists just don't want to work hard anymore. They want everything given to them on a silver platter. This has to be reversed.

As it is obvious that we are not going to be able to get a better class of tourist in the near future, we have to learn how to handle the type we currently have. In this vein we are proceeding to develop a tourist motivation program (TMP), with awards for those who actually improve their productivity. In the meantime you might want to cut back on your staff and advertising until we can reverse this trend.

It is very hard to make cases like these unrealistic. Both of the previous examples have their basis in fact. Things are not really managed very well.

A few years ago, I was helping a hotel chain recognize its need for improvement. Every 3 years the chain would bring all its managers, from all over the world, together for a review. As part of that process, I was asked to make a presentation. Instead of standing up and talking with them for an hour, I decided to give them a real example of the problem they had.

I wrote a speech for an actor to present in the role of a consultant. He was to say that we were preparing a program to teach guests to be more obedient and cooperative. It was really a very funny bit, and I felt like Woody Allen watching him deliver the material in a sincere and slightly pompous manner.

That is, I was delighted until I noticed that the audience was thrilled. The assembled managers believed that the actor was sincere and the program was genuine. It was obvious that they felt this was a step in the right direction. Afterward we held an open discussion, and they became downright hostile when they realized we had been putting them on.

This kind of misunderstanding happens because the participants in an organization have not been fully oriented on all the arrangements covered in Chapter 3. If they don't know the purpose and charter, as well as the other conceptual parts, then they might as well not exist.

Consider it from the leader's point of view. If the people do not know what is expected of them, the leader cannot plan on any specific occurrence. A sales manager, for example, can never know how customers are being treated or handled unless everyone involved understands the same thing.

ORIENTATION

New employees require at least 1 day of basic orientation and then a week or two of reminding. As stated before, all the necessary material can be inserted into their procedures manuals. But that is no guarantee it will be read. You have to read it to them—hopefully, in an interesting manner.

Older employees need reminding continually. Each Family Council or other group session should include at least one mention of the charter of the company and its purpose. Each speech should say something about the goals of the company.

SYSTEMS

How do we do all the functional things that make an organization go? The number of systems seems endless:

Purchasing	Travel
Accounting	Auditing
Marketing	Fund-raising
Payroll	Stock control
Invoicing	Hiring/firing
Benefits	Personnel Evaluation
Job descriptions	

And these represent just a few. Many are well documented, but most just exist. Systems are the communications center of the operation. No one can do everything by himself or herself. In fact, there is little one person can do without input or cooperation from another.

Unfortunately, most of the monitoring or controlling we do is aimed at the final product, whether that product is a piece of paper such as an insurance policy or hardware such as an automobile. These final units are examined in great detail, but the systems that put them together have free rein as long as the units are not obviously defective.

I think we need to be more concerned with *systems integrity* (SI). The purpose of SI is to examine existing systems to see whether they are doing the job, to insist that they become properly documented and described, and then to monitor conformance to the systems.

Systems integrity also includes internal audit and quality control. The results have been remarkable. People don't fight anymore about who is supposed to do what, and the amount of paperwork has actually decreased.

One aspect of this way of operating is the Product Integrity Board ("product" in its broadest terms). If a change is to be made in products or systems, or even in brochures of the organization, this board passes on it. The purpose is not to approve or disapprove, although the board can have that authority. The object is to let everyone know about the change so that it can be implemented properly.

COMMUNICATION

One inexhaustible subject for managers is communication. Somehow it never happens completely. Someone or something is always left out. Understanding is never quite total. The reason we don't do better is that all the activity is spent on transmission, with very little concern for reception.

Transmission, of course, refers to the logical communication activities conducted by business people: meetings, newsletters, press releases, conversations, memos, letters, signs, banners, cards, and all the other methods of giving a message to another person.

Reception refers to the listening part, which is what all the transmission components are supposed to excite. That is where we need to work. Nobody really listens—well, hardly anyone. I feel that listening is not a normal characteristic of the human being. It has to be learned. Classes should be conducted on how to listen. Just taking that step will cause a great deal of improvement. It will concentrate everyone's attention on the subject.

In the meantime, the transmission components need to be used correctly:

- *Meetings.* These do not need to be punishment. After all, gatherings to discuss a subject of common interest are what parties are all about. If the same group of people who couldn't get enough of each other at the company picnic are bored out of their skulls at the monthly status review, it is due to the attitude and the material. Meetings should never be uninteresting. With an agenda, prepared presentations, and a planned opportunity for participation, meetings can be anticipated with pleasure. The real key is to have them when they are necessary, not just when it is time to have them.

- *Newsletters, newspapers, etc.* Our company started its own official newspaper when it had only twelve employees. It is a four-page, professionally printed newspaper with photographs. It is the main source of what happens outside the business news of the company. People read it as long as it is interesting.

- *Organizationwide status reviews (or Family Councils).* Everyone should come together at least once a month for a discussion of what is going on.

- *Memorandums.* Establish patterns for writing memos; do not leave them to chance. Very few people write with enough clarity to be understood by the willing "listener," let alone the rest of us, who merely scan what should be digested.

- *Conversations.* Management has to get out and get around.

DEVELOPMENT

Somehow or other, each of us is expected to carve a personal way through his or her career. Individuals who are fortunate enough to have a wise person take an interest in them do much better than those who have to figure it all out for themselves.

The fact that most of us don't do for a living what we studied in school is an indication that help is needed. Development must be taken seriously.

The business world divides itself into professional and administrative areas. One group performs the revenue-causing or service-conducting tasks; the other runs the business. Both areas have career paths. Sometimes these paths intertwine, particularly at the top of the organization. Often we see a chairperson who came up through finance and a president who was in manufacturing.

In a development program the paths must be defined so that people can see where they can go. Then employees must be helped in two other ways.

First, people must know where they are now. They need reviews and consultations that let them discover their abilities and talents. They need to know how their performance compares with the performance of others.

Second, people must know how to bridge the gap between where they are now and where they want to go. They have to know about schooling, application, or whatever it will take to bring them up to the level of competence necessary for advancement. If they do not want to pursue the options, then they do not have to. But at least they have the choice.

I feel that organizations have an obligation to their employees to help them financially, as well as in other ways, in gaining the skills or knowledge they need. This is a good investment for companies because they obtain increased performance from an employee who is already oriented and trained.

There is no better way to reduce turnover and increase competence than to have a well-considered development program. It should be organized by the Human Resources department but monitored by the Executive Committee. Education, like war, is too important to leave entirely up to the professionals.

APPRECIATION

Nothing is more important for the leader than making certain that people who deserve appreciation receive it, yet this easy-to-give aspect of business life is often not handled very well. In a company where I used to work, the Quality Department solicited nominations worldwide for Ring of Quality awards. It was some time before we realized that this was the only corporate-wide recognition. We began to receive nominations for people who did not qualify from a quality achievement standpoint but obviously deserved appreciation for some other reason.

Appreciation should be part of the daily character of life. "Please" and "thank you" are taught to us as forms of polite social intercourse. The appreciation I am talking about is nothing much more than that. It is recognition that the person is real and has an identity. It is a public affirmation that the person is part of the operation.

When I visit a plant or an office of another company, I have no difficulty in knowing how the managers rate in this regard. As they show me around, either they introduce me to the employees or they do not. If they do not, then I do it myself.

Lack of appreciation is particularly evident in regard to workers in the lower levels of the organization. In my experience there are two different approaches when a guide (usually a senior executive) wants to show a guest how something is done.

In the first, they approach a desk, table, or bench where an employee is performing some task. The guide reaches into the area, picks up whatever is being worked on, explains the process, returns the work to its general location, and departs with the guest. The employee might as well have not been there.

When the guest asks about this, the guide usually responds that the employee would just as soon not be interrupted. But often the guest just receives a blank stare. People who give up their train seats to total strangers ignore their coworkers.

The other approach, which almost always happens in Japanese operations, involves introducing the employee to the guest. Then the employee is asked to provide a brief description of what is happening. The guest asks an interested question, and the guide makes a comment about what a fine job the employee is doing. Everyone parts feeling much better than before they met, yet the time elapsed is the same as in the first approach.

We need to give people plaques, certificates, and other formal recognition. That can be a part of the planned operation of the business. But a leader has to be a reflection of the soul of the organization. Each employee does not expect to be remembered personally out of the many people who work there, but he or she does expect to be treated like a person. The lack of such treatment is the most common complaint I hear.

The area where I hear it the most is the management group. Managers just do not receive appreciation. All they hear about is any lack of progress. I have worked for only two people in my career who did anything about encouragement at the managerial level.

Often this is why people change jobs. As one old boss of mine used to say to his subordinates, "If you need a lot of love, business is the wrong place to be."

It ain't necessarily necessary for it to be that way.

The above represents a brief tour through what the leader has to establish. One other aspect seems so obvious that I often have difficulty in getting senior executives to take it seriously. This is giving people permission to do their jobs correctly.

As leaders, we deal so often with the things that are happening incorrectly or have gone wrong or about to blow up that we forget to encourage the routine day-to-day functions that make the place run. Each time we change everything around in order to accommodate some crisis, we encourage people to fight and fix rather than to prevent and achieve.

We must learn to treat these crash actions as abnormal and the routine as normal. We must be as interested in one as in the other. We must not put roadblocks in the way.

For instance, in assembly-line operations it has always been a cardinal sin to stop the line. The idea is to keep producing. If something goes wrong, you can put a tag on it and fix it later. If the line does have to be stopped for some reason, everyone knows about it quickly. The person who stopped it better have a good reason.

This rule was established because it was recognized that if we don't produce anything, we don't have anything to sell. However, we are learning that the repair done off-line not only holds up product distribution but also does not teach us anything. We never get better.

Permission to do things correctly results in getting those line-stopping problems identified, corrected, and eliminated. Soon the operation flows smoothly. People are not burdened with simplistic rules and regulations from a bygone era. Their emphasis is on the complete picture. What we really need from an assembly operation is a steady flow of deliverable products, made defect-free and with ever-increasing productivity.

Gaining permission to do things right can be a lifelong frustration unless the leader thinks it is important too.

Chapter

5

Exampling

THE GRASSHOPPER AND THE ANT

The first thing Carl noticed about the restaurant was the crowd. It was clear to him that it was going to take a long time to eat lunch.

"We'd better go somewhere else, Sally," he said. "I'll be late for my afternoon appointments if we can't get out of here on time."

"Don't worry about it," Sally soothed. "I told Debbie when we made the reservation here that you could only give them an hour of your time. She said they could do it in 45 minutes flat if we told them what we wanted."

"What did you tell them?" asked Carl as they took their seats.

"Well, they make everything from scratch, you know. So I said whatever the fish special was, we'd take one each. I think it's halibut, but it will be the fresh fish the guy came around with this morning."

Carl unfolded his napkin, took a warm roll from the basket, and nodded. "I really appreciate that, Sally. A little efficiency and planning move things along. Most people don't do any preparation at all. That's why they never get anything accomplished."

"You're involved in a lot of things, aren't you?"

Carl sighed. "Too many, I guess. But I feel that we have a responsibility to participate in community activities as well as our own business tasks. Sometimes it gets a little overcrowded, but the satisfaction is worth it. I wind up working late at night in my den to get my company work done."

Debbie came by at that moment to see whether they were settled in and to bring two new tenants to the table.

"There's no room at the inn," said Debbie. "Can I seat these two orphans with you guys?"

"Certainly," said Sally. "We always have room for Jim and Marcia. This is a great surprise."

After much handshaking, hugging, and cheek nuzzling, the four friends settled down to the serious business of eating. Debbie included Jim and Marcia in the special order and assured Carl that it would not interfere with his exacting schedule.

"How many things are you involved in, Carl?" asked Sally. "Before you answer, I should explain to our tablemates here that we're discussing your schedule and how you have to plan everything so that it all comes out right."

"Well, I don't always get it right. That's why I have to rush so much."

Marcia smiled. "Let's see," she said, "I'm on the symphony board with you, and you're chairperson of the Patron's Committee, and I know that you head up the Indian Guides Council."

"And," interrupted Jim, "you're active in our church, with most of your emphasis going toward the stewardship drive. What else have you been working on?"

"Outside my company jobs, that's about all. There I have a corporate assignment to head up a committee formed to standardize the procedures manuals. But that's my only other interest."

Sally leaned forward. "So you have three community activities and one company assignment in addition to your job and family responsibilities? Don't you feel that's too many?"

"Not really. Each of you has as many or more, and from what I see, you handle them all without coming apart at the seams. In fact, as I think about it, I've never seen any of you rushing around or having limited time like I do."

The three smiled at Carl as he began to experience a dawning. "Are you three trying to tell me something? Is this whole lunch a setup?"

Sally blushed. "Well, we love you, and we thought there was something you might like to know. Did you ever hear the story of the grasshopper and the ant?"

"*The Grasshopper and the Ant*? Sure, we all had that in kindergarten. The grasshopper sang and danced and played all summer, while the ant trudged back and forth from the food source to his hole. When winter came, the grasshopper starved, while the ants lived to trudge another year."

"Actually," said Jim, "the ants bailed him out, so he didn't starve. But he didn't learn anything either."

"Well," smiled Carl, "we ants are a generous and helpful lot."

The other three sat silently looking at him.

After a long pause Carl looked thoughtfully from face to face. He was beginning to think that there was more to this discussion than he'd originally conceived.

"I am an ant, aren't I?" he asked.

It was Jim's turn to blush. "Remembering that we all love you and feel that you are one of the brightest and most energetic persons we know—you are a grasshopper in ant's clothing."

Carl reached for another roll and buttered it earnestly in order to cover his confusion. He had always considered himself a dynamic executive. Goofing off was something he never did.

"I don't mean 'grasshopper' in the sense of 'the world owes me a living,' like in the Disney film. What we are talking about is someone who works like crazy but never gets much finished in the process. People like that need a lot of help from their friends."

"For instance," muttered Carl.

"Let's take the Symphony Committee," said Marcia. "You

brought the committee together, developed a great plan for invitation letters to potential patrons, laid out a budget based on what was going to happen, and encouraged the hiring of a new assistant conductor. It was a great planning job."

"So what's grasshoppery about that?" asked Carl.

"Well, you insisted on writing the invitation letters so that the committee could have them printed and mailed."

Carl thought a moment. "I wanted them to have just the right touch. But I have to admit I haven't had time to get around to that. Let me mark it on my 'to do' list here in my pocket calendar. What's the schedule for sending out the letters?

"They went out last week," said Marcia. "We just ran out of time, so I wrote them. I left calls at your office all week long but never got a response."

"We were all wrapped up in the Procedures Committee meetings. I am going to have to write a complete procedure for writing procedures. I think I scheduled that for next week."

"Put your calendar away for a moment," said Jim. "I want to talk with you about the church stewardship drive."

"I'm giving my testimony on Sunday," said Carl. "We're really going to have a well-planned effort this time."

"That's true. It is well planned so far. You really do a good job of bringing out ideas and laying out strategies. Everyone is very excited about the whole process."

"Well," smiled Carl, "that's being an ant, isn't it?"

"Not really," sighed Jim. "Very little is actually happening because you've placed yourself right in the middle of all the things that have to be accomplished. No one can do anything until you finish the tasks you are supposed to do. Don't reach for your calendar. The fact is that the three items you wanted to complete don't exist."

Carl was disturbed. "I just wanted to be certain that the framework was correct. That's the only reason I wanted to write those personally."

Everyone nodded.

"We can understand that," said Marcia. "You have a better sense of these things than almost anyone else. The problem is, well, the problem is that you somehow or other never quite get them finished. Your intentions are great, your heart is in the right place, and as we said, 'We love you.' But you have to shed that grasshopper skin. It's driving us nuts picking up after you."

There was another silence.

"Let me see if I have this correct," said Carl. "You're saying, in between the times you assure me that you love me, that I start all kinds of things, take the key actions for myself, and then don't finish what I said I would do. Right?"

Everyone nodded.

"Since we all spend time together and work on various things together, you're concerned because it makes more work for you and also because you want people to think well of me. Is that right?" Carl looked from face to face.

Squirming a little in his seat, Jim nodded again and started to speak.

Carl held up his hand. "So you're saying that I'm a grasshopper because I work hard on things but never actually get finished, so the end result is that I might as well be playing around. Grasshoppers make a lot of work and trouble for ants."

"Well, they do add to the things that have to be carried into the nest," smiled Sally.

"What cure do you have for all of this?" asked Carl. "I don't want to spend my life making problems for everyone."

Marcia took a card from her jacket pocket. "We thought you might ask that question, so we put it all down on this card for you. It says two things: (1) Delegate with trust, and (2) Do my job now."

"I'm always concerned that people won't do the job right."

"Whether they do or not is a function of how well you explain it to them. When everyone understands it, all goes well. That's leadership," Marcia commented. "I've heard you say that many times."

"True, true," murmured Carl.

Sally reached across the table and patted Carl's hand. "Those symphony letters took me 15 minutes to write, and the committee had them printed and mailed in three days. You could have given us that job at the meeting."

Without any of the four noticing it, they had finished their meal and were sitting with coffee and the check. Carl was obviously pondering what he had learned.

"I think you're right," he said finally. "I have been rushing from project to project, scheduling everything but completing very little. I'm going to dump my calendar and just start the practice of finishing each thing as it comes along. That takes a great deal less time. Let me have that card.

"Do each of you have one of these?" he asked.

After a startled moment, Sally said, "Well, not really. We made it for you."

"Well, let's get some cards from Debbie right now and put these directions down for you. For all I know, you people might be closet grasshoppers."

Jim walked over to the restaurant desk and returned with three calling cards.

Carl distributed them with instructions that the two directions be written on each. "And I have a third one," he said. "Don't do anything twice."

"Gee," said Marcia, "that's a great addition to the list. What we're after is taking action that's final."

"Let me give you an example of that," said Carl. "I had planned to pay for the lunch today, but I only have a credit card. If I use it, then I will have to write a check next month when the bill comes. That would be doing something twice. So in the future, I am going to have to remember to bring enough cash with me. I will stop at the bank on the way home and take the proper action.

"In the meantime, you ants might want to chew up this bill."

Carl was called to account for his "witness." He was talking in one way and acting in another. What people saw him doing came through a lot stronger than what he said he was doing. Carl didn't really trust anyone to do things, yet he never quite got around to finishing them himself.

Some managers just can't let go, particularly those who become leaders. Many develop a terminal case of "big shot." They have to be the ones who do everything. As a result, it is not possible to know where they are in a process or what they are going to do next. Policies and procedures mean nothing to them. When cornered, they resort to something like, "Well, if I can't have the authority that goes with the job, then give it to someone else." They are difficult to deal with unless a little reason can turn them around the way it did Carl.

The whole matter of business ethics comes into play. The leader must be a walking, talking, visible example of what the ethics of the business are to be. Policies are useful, but example is all.

There is considerable evidence to show that today's managers bend more rules and take greater advantage of their position than managers in the past, but this is probably not true. Accurate understanding of bygone days fades with the passage of time. A lot of shady things went on then too, but on a much smaller scale. Yesterday's scandal is today's petty theft.

I have known thousands of people in business who worked at all levels of responsibility. As a quality management professional, I have conducted audits and evaluations by the hundreds. My relationship with the evaluation activity of many companies has supplied information that gives a clear picture of what, if anything, was happening.

Over the years, I have come to the conclusion that very few people will do something they consider wrong. The problem, particularly with white-collar crime, is that the definition of "wrong" varies in the minds of those involved. Their leaders make it so.

The entire work force of a large insurance company spent its time writing and issuing fake policies. An oil venture firm never drilled that first well and went to incredible lengths to cover up the swindle, with the cooperation of its employees. The firm even placed fake pipes around a borrowed garbage plant to show potential investors its "refinery."

Each day ordinary people swipe paper clips and other items from their companies. Corporations take advantage of the government; bartenders pocket some of the cash flow; and some fund-raisers take 80 percent and return only 20 percent to the charity. Scofflaws by the thousands refuse to pay parking tickets.

All of these are not necessarily the symptoms of a decaying morality. In most things people act in a responsible, caring manner. They pay bills and meet obligations—in personal life. The kind of things I am talking about are encouraged by the way businesses are run and by the regulations set up by the government and some customers.

One half, or more, of the workers in the United States today are in the administrative business. They do not create any wealth: they document and move transactions. Very little can be accomplished without recourse to accountants, lawyers, and other business professionals. All of this creates a world of information understood in its entirety by no one. It all is moved along somehow by people doing what they know about. Making this happen requires the development of procedures and regulations, both of which cost money. The $600 screwdrivers that the media gleefully attributes to contractor swindling really do cost $600. They may even cost more—the contractor may be embarrassed about charging the real amount. The tool itself probably costs under $10, but the paperwork and overhead run up the cost.

All of this is a matter of integrity and its lack. No one trusts other people, and everyone takes pains to let others know that. The regulations and requirements that go along with personal finance are enough to let us all know that. The microscopic print on the back of a loan form is enough to terrify anyone. All of this becomes a self-fulfilling prophecy. Customers ask for a clear description of any deviations in the product they ordered. The supplier sets up a department to do that. In manufacturing this is called *material review*. The more sophisticated version is *configuration control*.

When it is expected that people will not do what is planned, they don't do it. I often feel that the system of grading in school contributes to the lack of accomplishment. If we don't have to do it all, then we usually don't. There is a whole systematic exampling of lack of integrity:

- A "sold out" concert always has a few specially held house seats available—for a special price.
- The tables in a restaurant are not assigned on a first-come, first-served basis.
- Golfers don't always count everything.
- Banks give different rates to different folks.
- Farmers are paid for not planting crops.
- People don't read the forms they are required to spend so much time filling out.
- The experts are usually wrong.
- Insurance companies don't pay off what the loss is really worth.

Integrity is usually thought of in large terms, such as being true to the nation or not swiping the payroll or keeping one's word. It is not considered to apply to the things that everyone takes for granted. The late Fred Allen used to do a monologue about having the right to fill your fountain pen at the post office's inkwell. Obviously, that was some time ago: the problem has since been corrected by technology and the ballpoint pen (which is chained to the desk in the post office).

What I am getting around to here is that the leader has to create the integrity of the operation by personal example. Some places are shining examples of adherence to traditional values, while others bring back memories of the Dalton gang.

To construct a pattern that will help the leader cause integrity to flourish in the organization, consider the traditional small town. It is not necessary in that world to lock doors, put anything away, worry about crime, or distrust one's neighbor. The reason for this behavior does not lie with the police force, which tends to be rather casual about the whole thing. Nor does the explanation lie with the "kind of people" who live there. Small towns the world over have the same situation: if a crime is committed, the culprit will prove to be someone who was wandering through.

The simple reason is that the inhabitants all know each other, and their personal reputations with their neighbors are important to them. It is hard to go around mugging people when recognition is certain. The residents even notice when someone leaves town. In big cities, muggers and other thieves can roam in neighborhoods where they are not known.

People in an organization care about what the other people in that society think of them. They are not quite as concerned about the suppliers, customers, and regulators that affect the business. If they feel that the mode in that operation is to be loose and easy with the facts and funds, then they will conform to that style. They will encourage others who are naturally bent that way to join the group, and soon the entire organization will be cheerfully corrupt. The leader, noting that all hands are smiling and working, will assume no skulduggery is afoot.

Setting forth a list of commandments will not convince anyone that management is serious about integrity. Hanging a few pickpockets never did much to discourage that craft. In fact, the crowd that gathered for the ceremony was considered a proper target for other purse snatchers. Besides, for every rule there is an exception or a loophole that can be used to show no infraction was intended.

Integrity is as integrity does. The example set by managers comes across quickly and clearly. People expect those with big responsibilities to march to a slightly different drum, but they do not expect them to bend rules or take advantage of their position.

Remember: Almost everything that goes on in an organization is known by most people. With that in mind, here are some signs that will be picked up as permission to be dishonest about things:

- No one on the management team is around during the holiday season, when other people would have to take vacation time to be off.
- Expense reports for senior executives show that they never personally pay for anything they do during the week. (Believe me, this is general knowledge.)
- Company employees run errands for top managers, such as buying birthday presents for their spouses.

- Secretaries get coffee for executives.
- Executives park in the visitors' or no-parking slots so that they can run in quickly.
- Special customers get special prices.
- Time off during the week for golf or such without a customer is considered okay.
- Supervisors of all levels do not get to work on time.
- Lunch hours last more than an hour.
- Personal letters are mailed by the mail room.
- Jobs go to outsiders because it is easier to recruit than to develop and select.

I realize these don't sound like big deals in themselves, but they are the substance that weaves the web. A recent president had difficulty with subordinates who became overenthusiastic in conspiring against an opponent. When the entire operation came unglued, they were all surprised to learn that others felt this was not the way to act. They had been exampled to believe that it was within their rights to fool with the rights of others.

Leaders often just do not realize what they can cause if they permit the impression to exist that there is room for dishonesty in any form in their world. Fuses are lit all over the place. Who knows where they will lead?

Handling

Everyone expects the leader to be all things. The blame for lack of success will fall on those shoulders; some of the praise for success will reside there. It is not entirely fair, but it is pretty close. How well the leader survives the personal demands surrounding the job depends to a great extent on how matters are handled. Success, downtrends, change, statistics, and time are a few of the events that reach out to us for attention.

HANDLING CHANGE

In trying to develop a strategy for an organization, you need to provide a guide that can be used as a base for all future action. If you are going to establish branch offices in ten cities over the next 5 years, many things have to be accomplished. A clear strategy will let the various groups involved "plan their work and work their plan." Hardcover notebooks contain the well-thought-out results of off-site conferences held by top management. These are available to everyone and, in fact, are usually issued by serial number.

THE CASE OF THE GROWING HOSPITAL

Karl Valve, the hospital administrator, was having his regular Monday morning staff meeting. As the department heads gathered, he passed out the agenda for the upcoming trustees' meeting. Each month the board gathered to review the hospital's business and hear reports from the various committees of the board and the hospital itself.

As he moved around the table, Karl began talking. "The main item for the trustees to consider this month is the report of the Operations Committee on our expansion program. We are supposed to have already begun construction of the parking garage and the new 100-bed wing. The committee is concerned that we have been delayed."

Sally Thompson, the controller, nodded. "I guess a lot of that delay is my fault, Karl. We just have not been able to get the bids and the funding to line up together. The Wilkerson Foundation gift has to be matched by contributions from individuals. We have enough pledges, but the foundation wants to see cash."

Clyde East, her assistant, spoke up. "And the contractors have been stalling on getting their final bids in because interest rates have been dropping and they think they will get a better deal from the banks in a few weeks."

Karl nodded. "Nothing has changed. That's what it's like when it comes to running a not-for-profit organization. All the outside people think we don't have a time schedule."

"We are going to fall behind on the master plan," commented Clyde. "If this addition doesn't start soon, we will not be able to meet the demand that is expected 2 years from now."

"Let's look at the numbers," said Karl, motioning to Eleanor Rolls, the operations director.

The lights went down.

"Financial results this month are very much as had been

projected," said Eleanor. "Each of you has a printout from Finance. The interesting thing is that although our occupancy rate is off 4 percent, the financial results are about the same. People are having shorter stays in the hospital."

"Well, most of the revenue comes from the first 2 or 3 days, so I guess that makes sense," said Karl.

"There is one thing that doesn't make sense," said Eleanor, "and it just began to dawn on me as we were having that conversation a few moments ago."

She turned to her briefcase and pulled out some charts. "I have last month's graphics with me today because I was going to return them to Sally's office. Let me put them on the screen.

"This chart covers the last 6 months, and it shows a continual decline in occupancy rate. If this keeps up, in a couple of years we will have only about 60 percent of the bed patients we now have."

"That's interesting, Eleanor. But don't you think this might be a temporary situation? The hospital surveys all across the country show increased trends in the future—more people spending more time in the hospital."

"The population is aging," commented Clyde.

"Well, something is changing," said Eleanor. "All I was thinking is that if we are going to need fewer beds, we might not want to build a 100-bed addition."

"But it's in the master plan," said Clyde.

"If more people are needing medical attention and fewer are coming to the hospital, where are they going? said Sally.

Karl grunted. "There are a couple of interesting changes happening in medical care. Reading the literature and talking to other administrators indicates that some long-time ways of doing things are disappearing.

"For one thing, ever since the government started paying specific amounts of money for specific diagnoses, people have not been staying as long in the hospital.

"Then there has been the development of the short-stay surgery, where events that used to take 3 days or even a week now are walk-in, walk-out."

"Our outpatient clinic is the busiest part of the facility," said Eleanor.

"Right," noted Karl, "and the emergency room, which used to be the busiest, has dropped 25 percent."

"What does all that mean in terms of our new addition?" asked Sally. "It would seem to me that our master plan might be based on out-of-date assumptions."

"Looks that way," commented Karl. "The growth of neighborhood medical centers where you can just walk in and get most things taken care of has affected the normal practice of physicians. That's what is putting the emergency room under. Most of the cases that used to come in there weren't really urgent. They just couldn't get to their doctors.

"Let me get some information together, and we can chat about it later this afternoon. I think I should call the Planning Committee chairperson and ask for this to be discussed at Thursday's meeting."

Walker Burdett was not interested in changing the master plan. "Karl, we hired a strategy specialist; we all went away for a weekend; we looked at all the current information—in short, we did it right. That plan should last us for 5 more years.

"I realize that things change and some alterations might be necessary, but we will lose credibility with our donors if we do a big flip-flop and cancel that wing. Hospitals are always building wings."

Karl smiled. "I agree that we did it right, but the world changes and sometimes it does so rapidly. I've been an administrator for 20 years, and I've never seen anything like this."

"What is causing the changes?"

"My guess is that people are just tired of expensive medical care that takes a long time. They are tired of being regimented too, I guess. They want better, more detailed care at their convenience and with less investment."

"But it takes a long time to expand. Look at this place now. We have been adding on for 25 years. It's a jumble, but it works. We went through all this planning so that we could bring a little consistency to the place."

"And so far it has had a large effect. But I think we will make a big mistake if we don't take another look. What I see now is that we should look at the hospital as a resource to serve neighborhood clinics. We need to go out to the people."

"The medical staff is not going to be thrilled with that. They like people to come to the office and then to the hospital. We even built the new professional service buildings so that the larger admitters would be close to the buildings. What will happen there?"

"That should go right along. The hospital will still be the place to have major surgery, give birth, and recover from systemic illness. There will just be a lot less casual admittance and service. We will also probably have to double the size of the outpatient clinic."

"It seems to me that we should be able to plan better than this."

"Walker, you are in the insurance business. How well do your 5-year plans hold up?"

"Touché. We have to change continually, but most of that comes from what the companies do to us. But then again, they have to develop products that the customers want so that we can sell them. I guess it's much the same thing."

"Okay. But we are going to have a lot of trouble with the Wilkerson people. They had their hearts set on a wing that they could dedicate.

"Also, I can't believe the doctors are going to accept all of this very quickly."

"We will have to talk to them about it. If they could band together as a unit in order to make commitments, then we can work out a program. They will have to be more flexible when it comes to dealing with the patients, but it shouldn't hurt their business. In fact, it should help because if we don't learn how to change and manage the business properly, there is a good chance we might not survive."

Comment

Becoming locked into a plan is lazy management, but it takes so long to get everyone to agree on an overall approach that there is a tendency to want to avoid "making waves." Yet some waves will make themselves and show up unannounced, 15 feet high, right at the front door.

In managing change, figuring out what needs to be done is not the problem. That can usually be determined by looking at the result of current actions. Every management team bent on growing does that. Knowledge of the business or industry permits managers to see where they may be getting off the track or perhaps where an opportunity is presenting itself.

The history of wars shows that the general who was able to determine the need for change and execute it rapidly was the one who got his own way. Napoleon's troops were the best drilled in Europe.

To executives, change means that the proper people must know what is happening and must have an opportunity to state what they will need, if anything, in order to accomplish the change.

I would be willing to bet that the hospital management team will not get around to telling all those involved that there will be no Wilkerson wing until the first bill comes in.

When I worked in manufacturing in the dark ages before computers and PERT, we used to have a Change Board. Once a week (or more often, if necessary) we would gather in a conference room off the machine shop and go over changes. The engineering people would show us what they had determined needed to be altered on the product.

We would agree or disagree with them and come to some conclusion. We also had the opportunity to see whether the proper tools existed, whether the material was available, whether it would affect schedule, and so forth. There was a lot of yelling, screaming, and desk pounding, but the board was effective in its way.

I always wondered why we didn't do the same thing with regular management actions. One time I returned from 2 weeks on business in Europe to find strangers sitting in our office area. The whole department had moved to another floor without telling me. That gives you a real feeling of confidence.

Determining the need for change, executing the change, and

monitoring the success of the execution all require some formal communication system. Such a system only works when people take requirements seriously.

This points out the need for established systems of communication in every area and for a *systems integrity* function to monitor it all. We have to be able to count on one another. If people don't follow a system they have agreed on, then there is little chance of controlling change.

But the most important aspect is the open mind of the executive. If there is no continual looking around, sniffing to see whether the present course is proper, then the organization will inevitably run aground. At the same time, the basic principles and concepts of the organization have to be kept in mind. The hospital still plans to serve the same people, but it is reaching out to do so. It is adapting its traditions and practices to a new type of communication.

Banks have gone through the same transformation. I used to visit the bank lobby once a week or so; now I rarely go inside. I can get cash from a machine; I can deposit and transfer money by mail; and I can get a loan over the telephone. In fact, if you want to borrow enough, a bank representative will bring the papers to your office.

The actual implementation of change at the working level is done through supervisors who must form their own integrity meetings. If they all know what must happen, they will make it happen, and change will become a positive force rather than a disruptive one. Executives will never hear, "They don't know what they are doing up there"—even if they don't.

HANDLING STATISTICS

In order to manage a process properly, the executive needs to know what is happening. Sometimes the techniques of measurement and analysis become more complicated than the process itself. This often happens in the use of statistics. Statistics are a valuable tool in the hands of the professional, who really understands how to design experiments and arrange complicated data. However, drawing proper conclusions from statistics is a whole other matter. For instance, economists use statistics in great depth and complexity to put together the basic data for their analyses. But the answers they come up with are not necessarily what turns out to be true.

The control of a process, whether in manufacturing, service, or management, is accomplished by taking the pertinent information, looking for trends, and determining the reasons that those trends recurred. One way of explaining the action is to look at the annual physical data of a patient with the unimaginative name of John Doe. John is 43 years old. This is the third time that he has come to the clinic. After the doctors conduct his examination, they look at the numbers chart and this is what they see:

	1984	1985	1986
Age	40	41	42
Height	5'10"	5'10"	5'10"
Weight	185	190	195
Blood pressure	130/80	140/85	150/100
Temperature	98.6	98.6	98.6
Respiration	16	16	16
Cholesterol	89	140	215
Triglycerides	110	190	300

If you examine this data yourself, you will notice that several of the trends are upward. The numbers are getting higher. Blood pressure is rising; so is weight. What causes blood pressure to go up? One of the main things is weight. Another is the use of salt. Another is stress. Triglycerides and cholesterol are rising. What are the causes? Weight, stress, sugar (primarily alcohol), and general diet. The doctor, knowing all these things, can point out the fact that at John's present rate of progress, his size will approximately have doubled by the time he's 50.

Now, is the way to get John's process under control to teach him how to take a blood test, how to examine the blood serum for triglycerides, and how to count them? No. We have to look at the cause. What causes the weight increase that makes the triglycerides rise? What causes the stress? What produces the sugar?

John is doing no exercise and is eating as though he were 21. He needs to change his eating habits. He needs to go on a diet. His alcohol consumption is 6 ounces a day. That can be six bottles of beer, six glasses of wine, or six shots of whiskey. Whatever, it's too high. He needs to cut that down to no more than 2 ounces a day, and preferably he should quit altogether.

As for stress, John has had a recent promotion and he's struggling with the job. He needs to learn more about the job and get some counseling on how to do it better so that it doesn't bug him; perhaps he requires more education.

We have reviewed the measured characteristics of the process and identified the basic causes. This is what the use of statistics is all about.

What do we suggest for John's recuperation? To treat the blood pressure, we can put him on pills, but the pills are like a waiver. It's like permission to deviate: it doesn't eradicate the condition or fix it; it just compensates for it. John will have to go through life with high blood pressure and will always have to remember to take his pills. The pills make the body compensate, and they do that in an abnormal condition. What we really need to do is get his weight down, control his salt, and take other preventive measures. We know his blood pressure was not this way before.

We also need to get more statistics, since there may be a cardiovascular condition developing. An electrocardiogram will give us an indication of how the cardiovascular system is performing. If some specific evidence appears, we may go into more detail with other examinations.

This shows that the purpose of using statistics is to gather information in order to learn how to fix something.

Now what else shall we give John in the way of measurements and statistics? He now has instructions from his physicians concerning his diet, his physical exercise, and his check-ups. He is going to need a diet chart so that he can eat the proper foods. He is going to need a scale to weigh his food so that he is aware of how much he is eating.

He is also going to need a scale to weigh himself and a chart to document the weight, target, and pattern of reduction. We should give him a device to measure his blood pressure and teach him how to use it. Then he can take his blood pressure twice a day, mark it on the chart, and see where he's going. He should also have a timer so that he can keep track of how long he sits on the exercise machine or performs whatever exercise he's agreed to in order to get his pulmonary and cardiovascular systems working.

What we have done is set John up so that for his on-the-job work of health improvement, he has the tools for recording and keeping track of his progress. The doctor, as well as John, can look at these charts and see whether he is getting anywhere. If, for instance, in spite of all the dieting the patient is gaining weight, we have to go back and look at his patterns. He may not understand the job clearly and may be snacking, in the belief that doesn't have anything to do with it.

What we have now is statistics and the analysis of data being incorporated into a normal part of life. It is not necessary for the individual to understand vast concepts. It is only necessary to be able to do simple arithmetic and to plot a chart.

DEALING WITH TIME

When I first became an officer of a large corporation, I discovered that each and every officer received a copy of each and every telex sent by anyone in the corporation. That doesn't sound like much because most of us might expect to deal with a lifetime total of six telexes or telegrams. However, I received a stack each morning that contained at least 150 pink letter-sized pages. Then I realized that this was primarily a communication resource in this far-flung empire.

I sat in my rocking chair, put the pile on my lap, and started through them. After 30 minutes, it was apparent that some were interesting and some were not. They ranged from a plant's complete three-page weekly status report to a request from a New York traveler to be met at the Madrid airport. It was apparent that reading them every day was going to be a formidable task, particularly since I traveled half of the time. Mental calculation indicated that it would take only 6 unattended weeks to pack the office from wall to wall with pink paper.

It would not do to try to take my name off the distribution, since that would indicate a lack of interest. It is okay to be disinterested as long as that characteristic is not flaunted. So my secretary and I discussed the situation and arrived at the following disposition:

1. We would save the ones addressed to me and toss out the others. The telexes directed to my attention arrived in a special envelope and numbered about two a month.
2. We would instruct the entire quality operation worldwide never to use telexes, since they were somewhat less than private.

All of this worked out well for 12 years. Once in a while something that affected me would appear in a copy, but someone would always send it to my attention, circled and noted. That is one thing that can be depended upon: if you are supposed to do something, someone will tell you about it. The only problem was I didn't have a big stack of telexes to pore through while riding on the company plane. All I ever carried in my briefcase were the books I was reading. My biggest fear in traveling was to find myself on a long flight or visit with nothing interesting to read.

Time is life. We are allocated only so much of it; each moment is precious. What we would give to be able to return, if only for a few hours, to the momentous occasions in our lives. Older folks treasure each day; younger ones spend their days carelessly.

The mature person needs to recognize that there is time to do everything if the expenditure of this resource is carefully planned. That doesn't mean being the cartoon image of an efficiency expert, with stopwatch in hand. But it does mean thinking about communications and work practices.

Meetings are a waste of time. Everyone has said that. Yet it isn't true at all. Meetings are our friends. Properly arranged and conducted, meetings will add years of discretionary time to life. The problem with meetings is the way they are approached—as if they were isolated incidents in the life of the organization. Actually they should be viewed in the same light as mealtime. We eat for nourishment and energy. Each meal provides something to the "organization"; that is, our bodies and minds. Without them, or just eating on the run, we lose our strength and purpose.

But it is possible to eat a great deal and still not be nourished properly. The volume of food alone does not guarantee that each cell will receive what it requires to get its job done. Yet we know precisely what is required; we know how to prepare it; we know how to serve it attractively; and we know how to eat and digest the offering.

So why are there useless, dull, mind-boggling meetings?

Only because those responsible for these sessions have not taken them seriously enough to ensure that information and dialogue will be transmitted completely. They have not thought about the purpose of the meetings and the results they would like to accomplish.

I insist on an agenda for every meeting I attend, even if it isn't one in my company. Just making up an agenda provides confidence that the meeting will be useful. A starting time and an ending time are essential. The presenters should rehearse at least a little bit. An incredible number of responsible people cannot make even a semicoordinated speech, even though with some thought it really is a simple thing to do.

Visual aids are useful for supporting a presenter and essential for getting facts, such as financial numbers, up in front of everyone. But visual aids can also put the audience to sleep. Sometimes a speaker will write the speech on the aid, turn out the lights, and then read it to the group. I guarantee that will put them all out. Speakers do this because they think the information they are presenting is so important that it will override all other aspects.

The meetings of an organization have to be set up so that they support one another. Usually there is a staff or board meeting in which everyone responsible comes together to review current status, discuss new items, and hear special reports. This might take 1½ hours and should move along fluidly. Anything requiring additional information, evaluation, or action would go to the proper department or committee meeting.

Committees scare people too. Yet every well-run organization should have a committee for finance and one for operations, at least. The committees don't have to meet very often, but they do have to look at those subjects. Most organizations get into trouble financially because they don't know where their money is going before it goes. And the leader, wandering through the operation trying to keep everything in order, will soon create disorder. People have to know what is going on, not just what someone wants to do.

Executive time has to be looked at as something that is assigned, not just consumed. A little order never hurt anything. The problem is that executives continually react rather than act. The home manager is usually just dragged along by the events of the day, just like the head of a large corporation. Other people have control of their work activities.

I developed the habit of jotting my daily schedule down on a 3 × 5 card, which fit in my shirt pocket. That way I could know what commitments I had and plan my other work accordingly. That worked well for me. However, I found that others who tried this technique looked at it differently. They accepted the card in the morning from their secretary and then did whatever it said on the card. They called it a "dummy card." "Card for the dummy" might be a closer designation.

Time management is a result of making choices and assigning priorities. Those who schedule us need a list of priorities. Who comes first?

1. Family
2. Employees
3. Clients
4. Suppliers

5. Friends
6. Community

Given a list like this, first things tend to get put first. Without it, whoever calls in rides the pole. Managers who really manage arrange everything.

The big users of office time are mail and telephones. The common characteristic is that neither is controlled by the recipient. I have found that they can be brought to heel, given a little discipline.

Mail needs to be sorted by someone else into groups: things to read and answer, things to read, and other stuff. Take the "read and answer" group and look at each piece one at a time. Then either dictate an answer or forward it to someone else for handling. Do not put it anywhere until you have performed one of these actions. Do not put it in another pile on the corner of your desk. If an action does not come to mind, throw the piece out. (If you place it on the corner of the desk, it will get discarded in a couple of weeks anyway.)

If possible, get someone to highlight the "read" group with one of those yellow markers. Each of these pieces should be discarded or marked by you and forwarded to someone else for action or information. When I read a really good report (no more than 1½ pages and fact-filled), it gives me a charge.

The "other stuff" should be thumbed—while you are standing up—and dealt with immediately. For example, I sometimes like to know what is being advertised and how so that I can keep up with the technology in that area. Requests for contributions, on the other hand, should be channeled to the corporate secretary, where they can receive proper attention.

Mail processing should not take more than a half an hour each day, if that long. That is a long time to spend on things others originate, and it should be viewed as putting information in the personal memory bank. It also is a courtesy to those who have reached out to you in some way.

Telephones are about the only intrusion we pay to receive. It always bugs me when I have taken time to go to someone's office and he or she interrupts our conversation to take a call. I consider that very rude. I usually react by wandering around the office poking at things.

Calls should be sorted and noted. Then they can be returned on a planned basis. It is possible to sit and return a dozen calls in a half hour. Doing this personally is much more effective than having someone place the calls. I let everyone know that I am willing to talk to anyone who calls but it should be on my schedule. After all, it is my office.

Now there are going to be people whose call you would take anytime—spouse, grandchild, President of the United States. Take those happily, knowing that you are going to do whatever they want you to do.

Time management is all in the mind. It is much easier to react to whatever happens and then complain about it. But a little dedicated planning and personal consideration can produce a more effective manager.

HANDLING SUCCESS

"When it comes to quality in restaurants, this is where it all is—here at La Place. We have the greatest chef, the most magnificent menu, and the most fashionable clients. There is nothing like La Place."

Jon Sebal couldn't help crowing a bit. Mimi had just written a piece extolling the virtues of his establishment. It was an effervescent review, the kind she just never wrote. Nothing, it seemed, was wrong with the place.

"We will now be world-famous. Everyone will come here. Our wonderful food and service will be recognized. At last," he added.

"I am delighted with your happiness," said Georges, his financial backer. "I would be even happier if we were making some money. Last month we lost $125 on very good sales. We can only stand success like that for so long. If we are any more triumphant, we shall be on the bread line. They do not serve as well as you in that place."

"Patience, dear friend, patience," said Jon. "It takes time to build a quality establishment. Our reputation is growing. We will soon be making more money than you ever dreamed about."

Georges sighed. "I have to point out to you that we are full most of the time. Our biggest problem is finding professional staff. It is not possible to get a reservation in this restaurant for the next several days."

"What are you saying, Georges? Are you asking me to cut back on the quality? That I could never do. It is not possible. We have gained our present status from serving such quality. We have a duty to our patrons."

"No, no, I am not even suggesting that we eliminate even one small bit of our quality. I am not even asking to raise prices, although that would not be out of line. What I am saying is that we are serving all the people we can at this moment and we are not making any money. What good is a great review when no one else can get in and we are not profitable?"

"Well then, what do you suggest? We certainly cannot reduce the staff. There aren't that many of them as it is. We could stop the pension program and the medical plan, but I think the workers are counting on them. I hardly take any salary as it is, but I am willing to reduce that if necessary."

Georges patted his friend on the shoulder and calmed him. "Nothing quite so drastic at all. We just have to look at cost control. There must be somewhere we can reduce."

"Quality is not cheap; it costs a lot of money. You have to pay for it. We only get the best food, and the freshest. We prepare everything to order. The chef would leave us if we asked him to do less in that regard. Running a kitchen is a complicated business. It is very hard to reduce costs without purchasing cheaper food."

Georges shrugged. "We may not have any choice if we can't increase our profitability. At our present rate of 'success' we will have to close the doors in a few months. That will just give you time to get this new review framed and hung outside for people to see."

Jon sat down, distressed and unbelieving. "I am willing to try anything, but I am not going to explain to the chef that he must do things differently. He will leave and never return. Then we will be closed before we are broke. It is not an easy choice."

"Let us go back to the kitchen anyway. Perhaps we will find something that will help us make the correct decision."

At the kitchen door the chef greeted them with a concerned face. He was in what he called his "businessman's uniform," the smock he wore while working out menus and orders in his small office.

"I have been going over our costs and find that we are going to have to do something soon or we will be in trouble. We are not getting our money back from our investment. If we don't do something soon, I will have no place to prepare my meals."

He turned to Jon and raised an open palm. He was pleading for attention on the subject. Jon was startled.

"We have just determined the same thing," he said. "But Georges has been going over the books all day to come to that conclusion. How did you figure it out?"

The chef smiled proudly. "I have my own ways. I can determine almost exactly the price of an entrée. I imagine I should say 'cost' of an entrée or any other dish. That is how I select the menu prices to recommend. What has happened is that our costs have gone up in the past few weeks since we have been so busy."

Georges was puzzled. "But we are buying in larger volume all the time," he said. "Prices per plate should be going down, not up. What's wrong?"

"Most of it seems to come from training the assistant chefs. They use up a lot of food in the learning process. The sauce chef particularly has had a large expense in the past few weeks. But we have to be able to meet the demand. It takes quite a while to bring even experienced assistants up to our standards. They must learn just how I want it."

"But surely," said Georges, "they don't use the best food, the ingredients we plan for our customers, to train on. Can that be?"

The chef looked at him blankly. "But what else would they use? If they are to learn the style of our kitchen, they must work with the materials we use."

He was beginning to become a little indignant.

"What becomes of the food that is spoiled? For that matter, what becomes of the food that is acceptable?"

"In most cases," said the chef, "it is thrown away. Since our policy is to cook to order, we could not always be sure of what to do with something prepared for practice."

"Is there any difference in cooking something—say, meat—of the highest quality versus a little less expensive cut of the same meat?"

"Very little," nodded the chef. "It is a matter of technique that they are trying to learn. It is very much the same."

"And it is necessary to completely duplicate the dish whether it be appetizer, entrée, or dessert?"

"Do you mean, 'Do we have to make a big one, or will a little one do?' The answer is no. A little one will do fine. If we could cook just one bite, it would be sufficient."

"Then why," asked Georges, "are we using the most expensive material for people to practice on? Why don't we use less expensive things and teach in other ways? This policy will break us for sure. If we are duplicating the output of the kitchen and still serving all that we are serving, then we must have too many people back here."

The chef nodded in agreement. "Entirely too many. We could do very well with about one-third of what we have and cut back on the training. We could start a culinary school in another location and make money on it instead of trying to do it in our working kitchen."

"But why would we want to have a culinary school? And why are we trying to run one now? I feel that there is something I don't understand going on around here," said Jon. "I didn't know we were doing all this teaching. Where did that come from?"

The chef was puzzled. "But I was acting under your orders. You told me we had to obtain the very best assistant chefs, and the only way I could think of to do that was to train them myself. It has been hard, but they are coming along. In a few months they will be very useful."

Georges sat down. "Do they pay us anything?" he asked.

"We pay them," said the chef. "And, of course, we feed them."

"Would you mind if I fired them all?" asked Jon.

"Oh, I will be glad to do that for you. They are not very happy anyway. Most of them would like to go where they can practice on real customers instead of each other. They will be gone in the morning. This will help my costs a great deal."

As the chef turned back to his work, Jon and Georges looked at each other.

"It is apparent to me," said Georges, "that we did not do a good job defining our charter and purpose of business. If the chef was that far off, then we might have trouble in other areas."

"I will start on that while you recalculate our margins," said Jon. "Then tomorrow morning we can begin doing our management orientation properly. We will have to go back and find out what people think we are doing and then make clear what is actually going on."

"I can't believe it, but it is true. There is another large pile of money lying around here somewhere," said Georges. "We will have to start digging."

HANDLING THE DOWNS

"Into each life some rain must fall" is true of running an organization. There comes a time when reverses of one sort or another cause the operation to lose pace and begin to wiggle. It can be that competition has suddenly reared up. It can be an overexpansion that used reserve funds instead of cash flow. There are dozens of reasons, but they all come down to one basic fact: there is more money going out than coming in.

Even the best-monitored company can slide into this situation before realizing it. When it happens, specific action has to be taken.

1. Bring the management team together and do an autopsy on the status. The first requirement is to stop the bleeding and put a lock on the cash. Put a hold on all expansion. Identify the

commitments the organization has and cut back where legally possible. Stop hiring people. Don't buy anything new. Lower the level at which spending can be authorized so that this team knows where everything is. Get an immediate accounting of all assets. Do all this immediately.

2. Figure out what happened. Did something sneak up and bite management while it was paying attention to other things? Did some major customers or supporters delay their involvement? Are the accounts receivable behind? This is the time when you announce that there is no blame involved. The management team is responsible, so forget that part and get on with the survival exercise. "And we will survive."

3. Figure out what must be done to overcome the problem. How long will it take before revenues come up to speed? What is the difference between that and the necessary expenditures? If revenues are not going to return soon enough, then expenditures have to be reduced below that level for that period of time anyway.

It takes a long time to train people and to build a functioning organization. You don't want to disrupt that and lose good people. You don't want to solve the problem by just cutting the necessary expenses out of the payroll. That will eliminate future credibility. The employees will never trust management again. There are other ways: Everyone can go on a four-day week; that will reduce payroll 20 percent. Employees who leave for other reasons will not be replaced; raises and perks can be stopped; nonemployee costs can be stopped and eliminated if management works at it.

4. Talk to the bank or your financier about the problem. But make certain to have a solution and a plan that the executive team agrees on and is committed to complete. Financial suppliers get very nervous when asked to support overruns for "a little while."

Don't expect them to just ladle out unplanned funds. They will provide support without much bother for a brief cash-flow problem. But if the cure is going to take over 6 months and require significant money, they will want security. The assets of the company can be pledged, but in a young organization that might not be enough.

The personal property of the principals might have to be added to the pile. Nothing makes a banker think a borrower is sincere like having a lien on the old homestead. Before you make such a pledge, it is a good idea to look at the recovery unemotionally and make certain personally that it is going to be real.

Consider a stock offer if the company is public. Consider seeking a capital infusion from venture people. Consider everything except holding up a 24-hour market to get the money. Also, don't even think about taking it from someone who offers a shopping bag full of currency.

5. Talk to the employees about it. As soon as the situation becomes clear, bring the employees up to date. Ask them to not talk about it with others, particularly customers. They have to learn to be discreet too.

The employees are interested in being assured that whatever happens, their positions will be taken seriously. It is like waiting for a plane at the airport. Irritation sets in only when the airline doesn't tell the truth; its representatives keep giving optimistic reports even though they know it will be 4 hours until the flight leaves.

6. Set up crisis meetings on a weekly basis for overall actions and on a daily basis for team status. Keep minutes of these meetings, and be particularly careful about who is supposed to do what.

7. Go to your major customers and tell them about the cash-flow problem. Assure them that everything is going to be all right with their orders. Ask them whether there is anything you can do to increase your business with them, such as giving a discount in return for a long-range contract. If the products or services of the company are really important to them, they might even help with a loan. It doesn't hurt to ask. As long as a recovery plan is being implemented and the management team is facing the facts, a lot of support is available.

8. Go see your suppliers and ask them to help by deferring some of their charges and by letting their payments be postponed for a while. Offer to pay them interest on what is owed. Suppliers will usually hold still for 3 months in arrears as long as they see a plan and dedication. They will cooperate for a

year or so if they can get the cost of materials or fixed expenses back.

9. Reexamine the marketing plan. Get out and see your customers; find out what they think of the company. Look at new product development, and examine closely where the ideas are coming from. Is the company creating things for itself or for its customers?

One thing always is true in any organization: the organization will be successful if it provides what the customers want. It doesn't even have to be well managed if it has the right product. Customers will come in and take the item off the shelves or out of the desk drawers if the product is right.

The key is that the product must be right—and customers must know about it. The purpose of marketing plans is to let people know what is available and how it can help them.

10. Pray. The Lord takes a hand in the affairs of business when asked. Start each meeting with a word of thanks for taking the specific action that has been requested. Make Him a full partner and don't apologize for it to anyone.

This is all that got me through our brush with disaster in 1982.

When it is all over, remember what happened and how it came about. Tell the story to new executives as they arrive; remember it each year at a Family Council meeting. Learn from it, and the next time will never happen.

7

Doing

People do because they want to do. Helping them want to do is part of being a leader. But I have been learning that the usual ideas of what turns people on may not be all that right. Everyone wants improvement; everyone wants to do better; everyone wants to be well thought of. We don't hear much ranting and raving against success.

Yet not all that many people really accomplish a great deal. I have to wonder whether we really understand what makes it all happen. It seems to me that a lot more effort is put forth than is indicated by results.

"Productivity" is a good word. Few people agree on the exact meaning of the word, but I think we could accept something along the lines of "output for input." If we put in a dollar's worth of effort, do we realize at least that much in return? Of course we would like to get back more than the dollar invested; that is the way we make money.

Some countries, like some industries, do not return the cost of the doing. Those nations whose currency has dropped in value over the years are expending more than they put out. So if we have people who do $5 worth of work at a cost of $6, we must sink inevitably into the hole.

Many process industries such as textiles, steel, chemicals, and even oil have fallen into the trap of producing products that cannot be used as is. Many textile plants have a third of their output classified as "seconds." That means these products cannot be sold at a profit.

Not a good idea.

White-collar factories such as insurance offices, banks, and the government produce work in no relation to the demands of the market. It is only when catastrophe hits that corrective action takes place. Then herds of employees are fired, locations are closed, and economies are put back together for a while.

Companies take generations to recover from a shock like this. It seems to be only a matter of numbers, but it becomes a matter of credibility. People are not willing to put their hearts and souls into a temporary situation.

It seems to me that there are three phases involved in getting an organization or a person to be productive in the very best meaning of the word: *conviction, commitment,* and *conversion.*

Conviction is the intellectual decision that something is desirable to do. In this phase a person reads up on the subject, becomes interested in talking about it, and actually steps up output a little. Ten percent improvement is about the norm. Motivational activity in connection with the subject brings enthusiastic participation. The person has decided that the subject is worth doing and any support effort is appreciated.

I have a friend who is a great motivator. He does it for a living and is very successful. Whenever he comes to town, we have lunch and he gets me so churned up that I feel like going home and plowing up 40 acres. Considering that I don't have a farm, that action would have quite an effect on the neighborhood. One day when he was in the audience, I told a story about him. Pretend his name is Arthur.

I said that Arthur had asked me about my personal goals. "Is there something you have always wanted to do? Not be President or make a million dollars, but something very personal that you have never been able to accomplish?"

After thinking a moment, I said that there was something along that line.

"I like to play the Bay Hill golf course, the one Arnold Palmer owns. But the seventeenth hole is very difficult. It is a 185-yard carry over water to a tiny green that lies in the wrong direction. It is surrounded by sand on all sides.

"I have never made that green. Most of the time I am in the water; when I do get across, I am in the sand. Never on the green. It drives me nuts."

He was enthusiastic. "Your problem is that you have a low self-image when it comes to that hole. You just need to be more positive."

After a while he convinced me that I really could do it, and on impulse we drove out to the club and up to the seventeenth tee. It is right off one of the residential streets.

No one was around, so I opened the trunk of the car and took out a 3 iron, a tee, and an old ball. I marched up to the tee, put the ball down, and looked at Arthur.

He shook his head sadly. "Now Phil, you see here is your problem. You have an old ball on the tee. That shows a lack of confidence in your ability."

I was ashamed. I went back to the trunk and picked out a new black Titleist 100. Tossing the old ball aside, I replaced it with the new one.

"There, doesn't that feel better?" he said. "Now take a couple of practice swings."

I did that, giving it three of my best.

"Is that your regular swing?" he asked.

Smiling, I nodded.

"Maybe you better put the old ball back on the tee," he said.

Being motivated helps, but it doesn't take the place of knowing what you are doing. Sometimes we need more skills and information. But conviction is a good start.

Commitment occurs when we begin to get serious about something, serious enough to spend some money, give some time, take some effort.

"Is management really committed?" is the question consultants hear more than any other. It sounds like serious business, but commitment is really only the engagement-ring phase of things.

With commitment there is physical evidence that something may change. Managers are saying different things in their speeches and comments. The emphasis is changing. New machines or equipment may suddenly be authorized. Classes are held. New buzzwords appear.

When management genuinely becomes interested in changing its ways, there is an improvement of around 20 percent in whatever is affected. Most of this comes because people who have known about something that needed fixing have fixed it. Also, the attention paid to something that didn't have attention before just naturally causes improvement.

It is like a young man who decides the time has come for marriage. Having reached that conviction and accomplished the commitment, he suddenly begins to change for the better. His general appearance brightens up, and he begins taking better care of his clothes—perhaps acquiring some new ones.

From the time he got his own apartment until now, he probably ate most of his at-home meals standing over the sink. Suddenly he is involved in sit-down meals, learning how to carve meat, and having guests, other examples of a change in lifestyle.

Conversion is in the soul. When it happens, there never is any concern about going back to the old ways. When you walk into a factory run by those in the conversion phase, the housekeeping leaps up to grab you. The whole place is immaculate. The people have their noses to the grindstone and are enthusiastic about it. Output is high; waste is a memory.

How does one reach conversion? Through the experience of learning the better path. There are no pills. But the organization blossoms and sparkles, as do the people, as does the leader.

One nice thing about conversion is that everything comes naturally after that point.

Each year we have a black-tie dinner attended by all employees and their spouses. It is called the "picnic" for some forgotten reason. It really is a grand evening. There is a large band, a fine menu, camaraderie, and awards presentations.

One of the things I like to do is set up the table seatings so that people who normally don't spend much time together can get to know one another better. So each year I help lay out the table arrangements.

About 6 weeks before the last picnic, the switchboard operator came by to see me. She wanted to talk about the coming dinner. She didn't think the idea of assigned seating was that terrific.

"We want to sit with our friends," she stated.

Those who arrange the dinner were not thrilled with this thought, but I suggested that we just lay out a piece of paper for each table and let people form their own groups. We announced this at the Family Council, and after the meeting it took about 10 minutes to finalize the whole thing. All the guests had the best time they had ever experienced at the picnic. They are still talking about it. I was delighted.

My thought is that I went from commitment to conversion in the area of employee relations. I stopped treating them as if they needed my fatherly assistance and began dealing with them like peers.

It is the difference between my golf swing and that of a seasoned pro. The pro never thinks about hitting the ball, just where it is supposed to travel. I think about hitting the ball. It has not become natural to me.

In an organization, doing is causing people to have a productivity that makes everything happen on time and profitably. The attitude of doing comes from the leader's attitude.

Chapter

The GNU Story

"I really get frustrated. This company treats me as well as it can, and I am getting things accomplished."

His voice fell off.

"So what are you complaining about?" asked Caroline. "As far as I know, you get to do about anything you want to do, and we're making good money."

Rex nodded. As usual his wife made sense.

"I guess there are a couple of things, now that I think about it. And it could be a midlife crisis of sorts. But basically, I just want to be out on my own. I think I could take care of us."

"You have always taken care of us. I wouldn't worry about that. What are the 'couple of things'?"

"Well, I would like to be my own boss. Rise or fall on my own rather than work in an organization no matter how paternal. And second, I really think I could offer something to business that would make it all more efficient and successful."

"Would you want to have a big company?"

He smiled. "Oh, heavens no. Just you and I and some part-timers. We would have to have an accountant once in a while. I think we could get along quite well until we really got started."

"How about money?"

"A good and practical question. The kids are pretty much on their own, and we have some savings. I think that if we sold this house and moved to a less expensive area, we would have enough to see us through for a couple of years. We could not live at our present rate, of course."

"I thought it cost a lot of money to start a business."

Rex rose and walked over to his briefcase. He took out some charts and arranged them on the table.

"It depends on the business. I want to start a consulting firm that specializes in supporting the purchasing operations of middle-sized companies. We would need some computers and software, but I think we can lease about everything we will need. If I can arrange a couple of deals, we will be able to make enough to pay as we go along."

"How about venture capitalists?"

"The way that works now, they want the whole company. I am not about to trade a boss I know for a boss I don't know. If we were going into products, we wouldn't have any choice; we'd have to raise a couple of million anyway. We can start this company on our own. If we don't make it, then I suspect I can always go back to Lightblue."

Caroline smiled and patted his hand. "I've gone along with you all these years and it has always worked out. There is no reason I can't go back to work if that would help."

"You're probably going to have to be our whole office. We'll be in this thing together."

"So what's the first step?"

"Well, I'm going to ask a couple of old friends for advice, and then I'll tell the boss I'm leaving."

"What is this service?"

"Smaller companies can't afford to have a bunch of purchasing agents, and there really aren't any consultants in that field. Even though purchasing accounts for about half the money spent in this country, it is rather unsophisticated.

"What I want to do is provide these companies with a computer hookup where they can find out who sells what and make a connection. For routine things they can even place orders that way."

"Purchasing department for the nation?"

"That would be a great company name."

Caroline busied herself with a new pot of coffee. Despite her brave air this was quite disturbing for her. The thoughts of selling the house and moving to some indefinable somewhere were not easily assimilated.

She stopped herself from asking why they would have to leave all this, realizing that there would be time later for such a discussion.

"What do you want to call the company? Have you thought of a name?"

" 'Rex Diamond and Associates, Inc.' popped into my head, but since we'll never have any associates, I thought something simple like 'The GNU Company' would do."

She turned from the counter. "What in heaven's name does GNU stand for? I thought that was some African antelope."

Rex giggled and showed her a page from his notebook. "Generating New Understanding, how about that?"

"Interesting."

"We'll probably have to have seminars as well as in-house instruction. I think the service will market itself. So it just seems to me we'll need a very positive name."

"I agree."

"Tomorrow I'm going to have lunch with Jerry Watson. His company does about $100 million, and I know he has been having some purchasing problems. If he goes along, we'll be on our way. You might want to talk to our favorite broker and get an idea of what this place is worth."

The next day Rex and Jerry did meet for lunch and, following their custom, flipped a coin at the front door to see who would serve as host.

Rex lost and patted his friend on the shoulder. "This will be on me personally today because I'm not talking business for Lightblue on my lunch hour. I want to discuss something that I've been thinking about for a while."

As they checked their coats, Jerry smiled knowingly.

"If you're going to tell me that you've decided to chuck it all and set up your own business, that would be no surprise. I've seen it coming for some time. Let's sit over here by the window."

Rex was startled. "How did you know?"

"The signs are plain to one who has had the same type of yearning for the past 2 years. I can't do much about it because I have three in college. But after that, well, you never know. Tell me what you're thinking about."

Rex explained his plan in much the same manner as he had to Caroline. Jerry nodded encouragingly all the while. Then he spoke up.

"We certainly would be interested in being your first client, Rex, not to do you a favor but to help ourselves. We are having a difficult time in Purchasing. But before we get into that, let me ask you how your company is going to be different from any other one. Do you have a clear charter and purpose in mind? How are you going to treat your employees so that they will feel positive about the company? How are you going to run it so that it doesn't get like all the rest?"

"I don't plan to have any employees."

"You are going to have a bunch, and you will have a good-sized company before you are through. I repeat, how are you going to explain your understanding of the company's culture to the others who will join you?"

"I think you are out of your head, but if you are willing to ask your people to think about hiring GNU, then I'm willing to give this some thought."

Jerry tapped the table. "You're on. Now here is a paper that lists the things you should get straight before going further. By the way, have you thought about talking to Hal Lawrence and Tom Gibbons? I was with them last week and they are having purchasing problems too. Let's eat; I only get an hour."

Rex read aloud to himself. "Charter, purpose, requirements, dedication, attitude."

Rex had always respected his friend's ability to separate the essential from the ordinary. That is why he read the article entitled "The Role of the Leader" so carefully. However, it did seem to him that all this attention, prior to having something real, was premature.

But it couldn't hurt and he was getting tired of trying to make all the numbers come out properly. Squeezing 2 years of living out of 6 months of savings was not going to be easy. The company had to pay for itself from the beginning, even if Rex didn't have any income at all.

That afternoon he reviewed the items on Jerry's list. He began by writing a charter.

CHARTER OF THE GNU COMPANY

GNU will serve the managements of manufacturing and service companies by providing them with professional services in the purchasing field. We will act as their agents in direct buying; we will conduct seminars to instruct their personnel on the concepts and techniques of purchasing; and we will provide computerized reference and actual buying services to give our clients access to thousands of potential suppliers.

"That's kind of a statement of business," thought Rex. "It seems clear enough."

Just to make certain that it was clear, he asked Caroline to read it. She glanced over the page, handed it back, and commented that it didn't say anything about people—employee-type people. After all, she was supposed to become a GNU employee herself soon.

This really puzzled Rex. He planned to take good care of those who threw in their lot with him. Was it really necessary to get into all that? Apparently, even the best of intentions could be misunderstood. So he added:

GNU will be an equal-opportunity employer providing its employees with compensation, benefits, and consideration that can serve as an example to other companies. It will provide clear career paths and help employees grow to their potential. GNU will be a financially conservative company, borrowing only as needed, being fully audited, and paying its obligations as agreed.

Next, Rex worked on his company's purpose.

PURPOSE OF THE GNU COMPANY

GNU will exist to help clients, suppliers, and employees have productive, well-based lives. By making clients and suppliers more profitable, their businesses will become more sound. GNU will be a responsible community citizen.

Enough? Well, it seemed to be. "Perhaps," Rex thought, "any additional data required will be more obvious after a while."

The next item was requirements. Rex finally determined that this was the description used to explain to new employees (and to remind the senior people) just what the company did for a living and what each of the employees was supposed to do for himself or herself.

While this mental exercise was progressing, Jerry called to say that his company was definitely interested and that if Rex would send in a proposal, they could get something going. That made up his mind for him. He asked for an appointment to see Howard Teller, the Lightblue president. It was set up for the next morning. It was one thing to dream a little on your employer's time but quite another to be working on a different business entirely.

Howard was not pleased. "Why do you want to leave? You can do all that here. We have as many problems in Purchasing as anyone else. We can use your help on that. I can probably get you a new title and some more money. Just set up what you plan right here and run it. It's a hard old world out there."

"I know. I've given it a great deal of thought, Howard." Rex was getting a little nervous.

"You'll be giving up your pension and a lot of potential earnings, and there is no way I can give you any business for a couple of years. It would be thought of as encouraging others to do the same thing."

Howard stopped and looked at Rex. "I guess you've made up your mind, old buddy. I think it takes a great deal of courage to go off on a venture like this, and you have it. If you want to come back someday, we'll do our best for you. Your reputation here has always been excellent, and we'll keep it that way."

He stood and offered Rex his hand.

Out in the hall the doubts suddenly pounced on Rex, but it was too late now. He was committed.

GNU was going to happen. It was.

Rex turned from the calculator and aimed his pencil in Caroline's general direction.

"The key to getting established is the income we will receive from lectures and from explaining to potential clients what we do. I figure we can charge $500 a day and expenses for these sessions. That will bring us close to the breakeven point."

"You are going to charge for sales calls?"

"We don't make sales calls. A consulting day is a consulting day. Really, I think that potential clients don't take seriously what they get for free. After all, they are all getting paid for the meeting, and I am providing them with some valuable information."

Caroline nodded. "That makes sense. How many of these will you be doing?"

"Probably about five or six a month until we actually get some clients on retainer. But then I suspect I'll have to do them continually if we are going to grow. How am I going to teach a seminar, work with clients, and still make speeches? I really don't want to hire any people."

"I'm sure we are going to have to hire some people, which means we'll have to pay them, which means we can't start out in the hole. How come it's necessary to have fees that don't let us do better than break even? Why can't you charge what you have to charge? It isn't that big a difference, and it surely can't be that important to a company that's talking about millions of dollars in purchasing problems."

She turned to look at him as Rex absorbed this thought.

"I guess it's very elementary that you don't deliver a product at a loss," she continued. "But I don't like the idea of charging expenses. That gets the client involved in where you are going to sit on the airplane, what hotel you are in, and what the menu is for dinner. When you travel with me, some clerk is going to question my room rate. That's the kind of stuff that used to drive me nuts in my old company.

"Why don't you set a fee that covers expenses and then

charge them that and pay your own way? They would probably like it, since it's a much neater way of doing business."

Rex turned to the calculator and punched away. "That would come out to $1250. We could pay for the trip and our overhead and still have about $200 we could use for growing. But if our whole income is going to be derived from my trips, then we are going to be in deep trouble if I ever get the flu. We are going to have to start thinking bigger."

Rex parked his rental car in the visitors' area and walked the 60 yards to the front door of the massive building. Entering, he appeared to be casual and comfortable, but his inner voice was telling him to get back in the car and beat it.

The receptionist asked him to wait for a few moments while Mr. Ellison's assistant came down to get him. Sam Ellison was the purchasing director for Anson Corporation. Anson was a producer of industrial products and had six different divisions across the nation. Its revenues were right at $500 million a year, split rather equally between those divisions. Anson did very little international work.

Rex had been invited to come to Anson by Hal Lewson, who had read a paper that Rex had written; Hal then checked him out with the president of Lightblue and Jerry Watson. Ellison, who would be Rex's host, had set up today's meeting.

"You will be talking informally with Hal and me, as well as with Jim Jasper, my boss, who is in charge of the manufacturing staffs, and with José Garcia, the vice chairman, who runs Finance, Treasury, and Legal," said Sam Ellison as he motioned Rex to a chair.

"Is there any special equipment you will need?"

Rex shook his head. "I think not. Perhaps a blackboard if we get around to drawing a line or two."

"There is one of those in the room." Sam shifted in his chair.

"I've been interested in meeting you so that we could talk about some of your thoughts on purchasing. Most of the work you have done has been in service-oriented companies, hasn't it? Do these things apply to manufacturing operations like ours? For instance, we use a lot of castings and forgings. All of that is an inexact science; there aren't even drawings on some of those we have used for years. This is a judgment business.

"I understand you feel that parts can come directly from the supplier to the assembly area without even going through inspection. I don't see how that would be possible unless we put teams of inspectors in the supplier's plants. Our costs are tough to handle now."

Rex was nodding and following Sam's discussions while his mind was saying: "This is going to be tougher than I thought. Each new client is going to need a brain transplant before I am going to get anywhere."

But he responded to Sam's comments. "Actually, what we need to do is to get the requirements clear between ourselves and the supplier and then help the supplier produce defect-free units. That way there is no inspection needed, and the complete cost will be much lower."

Sam didn't appear convinced. "Most of these outfits have very few controls. It would take a miracle to change them. Let's go on into the meeting; we can grab a cup of coffee as everyone arrives."

During the 2-hour meeting, the executives in attendance showed that they were serious about improving their purchasing efficiency. After satisfying themselves about Rex's personal qualifications, they raised the question of how he would plan to provide the necessary education and support for their company. He had only himself, and there were hundreds of people involved in the purchasing activities.

"Senior management would also have to understand what was happening and be part of the participation," said Rex. "I think we can make it all come out right if we can do a couple of things. First, I will set up and conduct a 1-week class for Purchasing managers. We can take about fifteen at a time. We can also conduct a class for senior managers—with not as much nuts and bolts—but they have to comprehend the concepts and their role in making them happen."

"Where would these courses be?" asked José. "Could we hold them in one of our training rooms?"

"I would prefer to hold them at our shop, José," replied Rex. "If we let these managers come to class on site, they will be running their departments on the telephone during the breaks. We need to get their minds on these concepts and techniques and keep them there."

"What are you going to teach them? After all, these are all experienced Purchasing managers," said Sam.

"I just want them to take another look at the subject, one they might not ever see if they are wrapped up in the job every day. We will start off with concepts. There are three basics that involve effective purchasing:

"First, requirements must be understood in the same way by the purchaser and the supplier.

"Second, the performance standard must be that we will receive defect-free products from the supplier.

"Third, effectiveness will be measured by the cost of ownership. How much do we spend for the purchase, the storage, the repair, the warranty, the inspection, and the other aspects of ownership and use?"

"Then the managers will receive some implementation guidance?" asked José.

"Yes, I've prepared a process guide that will help them make these things happen. One step, of course, is to bring the suppliers in and explain their role to them. I will teach Anson to conduct supplier clinics. I see GNU's job as putting Anson in the Purchasing management business and serving as a resource while you implement."

"You are talking about a mind change, Rex. A lot of us have been at this for a long time and may not want to change. Do you think all of this will be a big shock to our people?" asked Sam.

"I think we will find that they are searching for a way of preventing the problems which bug them every day and that they feel management does not give them permission to take the necessary steps," replied Rex.

Hal looked around the table questioningly. "Obviously, we can't expect Rex to educate all of us in a couple of hours, but I feel there is certainly interest here. Rex, can we ask you to work out a proposal for us?"

Rex nodded in agreement. "If Sam could give me some time, I think I could present you with a strategy. I would like to have the opportunity to visit one or two of your divisions before laying it out. I need to get a better feel of how the people of Anson look at things."

"There are three operations that can be covered well in 2 days," said Sam. "Let's check schedules and see whether we can get there in the next couple of weeks. I'll go along if you wish, or I can arrange for you to go by yourself."

"I would appreciate it very much if you would lead me through the operations," said Rex, meaning it.

"OK," said Hal. "We'll all get back together when you two have a strategy to propose."

He put his hand on Rex's shoulder. "We are a stodgy outfit that has had its market all to itself for a long while. Now we are getting competition, and it is beginning to hurt. We have to learn to produce much more efficiently, and Purchasing is one of the major areas that we worry about. Everything else we hear has to do with ways of shaving the price. We don't feel we should make money out of our suppliers, but we really don't know what to do to make a dramatic improvement. We hope you can help us."

Rex felt as if he could get home an hour ahead of the plane if he could just get outside the cabin walls. He had actually been taken seriously by a company that didn't even really know him. Perhaps GNU would happen after all.

What was he going to write the proposal on? He only had some letterhead stationery, and it wasn't very fancy. He pulled out his pad and began sketching. Dealing with the printer would require a whole day just to design a form, and it would never be printed in time to present in a week or two.

Where was he going to hold classes? What was he going to teach? His basic concept speech took about an hour, and the managers could ask questions for another hour. What would he do for the rest of the week?

How many people in a class? How much to charge for the classes? The participants would want notebooks or something to carry home. There were no slides or charts or anything, only his knowledge and experience and beliefs.

There was work to do and he was going to need some help. At that moment Rex decided that he was going to ask for divine assistance and include the Lord in his company. From then on things got clearer.

Wally Thompson was not very surprised to hear from Rex. "I thought you might be getting hold of me when you figured you were actually running into some real problems. What's up, Doc?"

"I am at the point where I am actually going to have to deliver for a client and turn GNU into a real business. I need help. How about coming with me? I think I can pay you about two-thirds of what you are making, but we will get you some stock and it will be interesting."

"Do you have any clients yet?" Wally shot back. "Do you have any money? Do you have a business plan?"

"None of the above."

"Okay, I'll come. It will take me a couple of weeks to get out of here. Is there anything you want me to work on in the meantime?"

Rex smiled into the phone. "There sure is. We are going to have a seminar that I think will take about 4½ days. I have the first 2 days and the last day thought out. We need a case history to work on during the middle days; one that will let them deal with the concepts and techniques that are taught the first 2 days. It will have to be participation-oriented."

"No problem, I'll start working. How about moving allowance?"

"Three months' pay and you take care of the IRS?"

"Done."

Sitting across the desk from his lawyer, Rex was beginning to feel as if the world was becoming a very complicated place.

"I haven't had time to do any real work these past 2 weeks. Outside of visiting a couple of client plants and working out a strategy, I've spent the time on administrative things. It's wearing."

"What kind of things?" asked Henry.

"Well, insurance for one. We need health insurance now that we are becoming a five-person company. I hired a secretary and two associates, and that leads to a pension fund. We wili wind up with a defined benefit program that should give everyone about half his or her compensation at age 65.

"Listen to me talk: 'age 65.' I am beginning to sound like one of them. All of this represents a large commitment, but I've told the new employees the purpose and charter of the company, and that's part of it."

"It's most unusual to be so up-front with people, particularly in a new company."

"Well, I think that the company owes its employees something and vice versa. I hope that by getting these things clear, we will reach a mutual commitment that makes the operation function smoothly. It's more fun too when no one is feeling put upon.

Henry nodded. "It does make for consistency. How are you going to keep everyone this close when the company gets bigger?"

"I guess we will just work harder at it. We can all get together, in one room, as long as we are in the same town. The Civic Center holds 10,000 people if we ever get that large.

"If we wind up spread all over the world, we will just have more meetings. I'll go see them, but right now we can do it in my office, which is also my den. We need some room. I have been looking in the paper for space, but I need help. Do you know any good realtors, builders, building owners, or whatever?"

Henry smiled. "I know a fellow with the unlikely name of Bob Smith, who owns a half-dozen buildings. He has a couple that he's renovating right now. You might get together with him. I'll call him and inform him that you plan to make contact."

"Do it right now, and let's make an appointment for this afternoon. I have to go see the hotel people this morning."

Henry called Bob, who agreed to meet with Rex at Smith's office around 2 P.M. "He said he had a building that would be 'just perfect.' But it usually works out that way too," noted the attorney.

After thanking Henry for his help, Rex left to keep his appointment at the hotel.

The Lanier Hotel had seen better days, but it was clean and the facilities were usable. Rex wanted to reserve rooms for the managers who would be coming to class and a meeting room large enough for the group to use for a week, and he wanted to make arrangements for at least one lunch. He was beginning to feel that if he could schedule two classes a month, everything would come off properly.

Howard Allison, the hotel manager, came out of his office to greet Rex. As Rex explained his needs in the hallway, he could see that Allison was not too sure about it all.

"That's a lot of commitment on our part, Mr. Diamond," said the manager. "If you figure twenty-two bedrooms for five nights each, and our main conference room tied up for a week, and do the same thing a week later, well, it would be a big risk on our part."

Rex was stunned. "But isn't that what you do? I mean, you rent rooms out to organizations and people, don't you? I thought you would be delighted to have such a good bunch of business dropped in your lap. What's the problem?"

Allison glanced at his shoes. "Well, we don't really know you, Mr. Diamond. If you want to make this arrangement, we would expect a 50 percent nonrefundable deposit, at least 1 month in advance."

Rex blushed. "I find that hard to believe. I am certain that I could call any other hotel in town and they would be glad to do it. I would make all the reservations on my credit card, but the individuals will be paying for their own rooms. We will pay for the meeting room and the lunches."

The manager nodded. "We could arrange to put the lunches on your card a week in advance. That way we would be paid before they were served."

Rex stared at the man and then smiled thinly. "Let's just forget it, Mr. Allison. Thank you for your time."

Walking nobly out the door, Rex realized that although the

man was certainly uncooperative, he really didn't know Rex from third base. If he was going to deal with local merchants, he was going to have to get some local references. At least Bob Smith would want to know more about him. Rex hoped that Bob would have the right space.

So Rex stopped in the bank and asked to see the president, who turned out to be a friendly, likable person named Bob Wilson.

"I am just going over to the restaurant next door for a bite of lunch with two of my directors. How about coming along with me? We have heard about your new business and would like to know more. It may turn out that we can be of assistance to you in getting it off the ground."

Rex allowed himself to be persuaded and soon was meeting two gray-haired gentlemen who appeared delighted to have company for lunch.

"All Bob ever wants to talk about is bank business when he gets us to these luncheons," said one.

"We would like to hear what you are up to. Do you have a bank yet?"

"Not yet," said Rex. "We have just moved here; everything is happening so fast that I haven't had time to do much except lay out the charter and purpose of the company and line up our first client. At 2 P.M., I am meeting with Bob Smith to see whether he has some space for our office and classes. In the meantime, I am working out of my house and trying to rent classroom space in a hotel."

"Well, you'll need a bank. I'll have Hilary Swant get in touch with you. She can handle both corporate and personal accounts. What hotel are you dealing with?"

"None. I went over to the Lanier this morning, but they were not able to take care of me."

"I don't know why not," said one director. "I happen to know that their occupancy rate is about 45 percent. They're in a lot of trouble." He turned to Bob, "Do we have any money in there?"

"No," said Bob. "It's family-owned, and as far as I know, they have never borrowed from anyone. The hotel needs some work though. One of these days something will have to be done."

He looked at Rex. "Have you talked to Jerry Thompson at the Westside? He's trying to build up a business and would be very happy with a client like you. I'll give him a call and introduce you. Come to think of it, I don't know the name of your company."

Rex smiled. "GNU. 'Generating New Understanding.' It can hardly be called a company yet. There are only five of us, and we have very little income."

"What will be your product?"

"We are a mangement consulting firm, dealing with purchasing. We help clients learn to do it right. We will provide education for their managers and then a little hands-on help while they put it all together. Most companies do a very poor job of running purchasing, and they know it."

"You mentioned a charter and a purpose. What you just explained sounds like a charter. What is the purpose? I always thought the purpose of a company was to make money."

Rex smiled. "That is the traditional view, and certainly a company that plans to survive and grow needs to make a profit. We plan to do that, but we feel that the purpose of the company is to help people have lives. Providing jobs, a work interest, a cash flow to the community, and doing some good in the process, are basically what the company is all about."

There was a moment of silence.

"I never did get to ask you," said Bob, "what brought you around to the bank this morning? I don't want to send you off without seeing to your request."

Rex laughed. "I guess I was looking for someone to introduce me to the local merchants so that they would do business with us. I still need a hotel and a couple of restaurants, and I need to establish a bank account and a line of credit. To date we have been operating out of my checkbook from my old bank."

"You will never get that money back," cautioned a director. "One day you will have a controller and auditors, and you will say something about the thousands of dollars you spent personally on expenses, and they will look right through you. Be more formal."

Rex took the advice to heart. He was introduced to Hilary Swant, and they arranged to meet later in the week.

Bob Smith proved to be an interesting study in himself—tall, gangly, wearing cowboy boots, but pale from lack of sun. He threw his arm around Rex's shoulder and drew him toward his pickup truck.

"Let's go over to this building we're converting. If you think you are going to need room to grow, then you are probably going to need about 3000 square feet. We're just converting this place, and it will be done in about 4 months. You can have as much as you want and arrange it in any way you want."

As they careened down the side street, Rex was struck by the intensity that Bob projected.

"Do you have a ranch, Bob?" he asked.

"No, we live in an apartment over the shoe store back there. The kids are out on their own, so Alice and I decided we would live where we didn't have to drive all the time. I don't have any horses either, and I hardly ever go out in the sun. It blisters my face. Everyone teases me about these boots, but they're just the most comfortable things I've found to wear. Here's the building. It's right down the road from the Westside Inn."

"Perfect," thought Rex.

Workers were scrambling around the one-story building. Bob took Rex around to the bed of the truck and spread out plans for the building. Jabbing his finger, he showed the layout and then led the way inside.

"How much is the rent?" asked Rex.

"We would like a 3-year lease at $6 per square foot."

Mentally, Rex worked that out to $1500 a month. "How about utilities?"

"We can work that either way, but if there are several tenants, it can get complicated. Usually I just suggest that we add another dollar per square foot and I'll pay the utilities."

Looking at the space, Rex could see that a proper classroom would take up about half the area he was thinking about. Four offices and some clerical space would fill up the rest. A closet for material and a place for the students to have coffee would be out of the question.

"How about 4000 square feet?"

"No problem. I'll reserve it, and we can sit down with my architect later this week to design the layout. I see that you make up your mind right away. I like that."

Rex was feeling a little weak. This was going to take a great deal of his planned income, and he would still have other expenses.

"We'll put up the walls and door wherever you want them, and we'll put carpet on the floor. Anything else will have to be paid for by GNU. We'll work it out."

It felt good to have his company called by a real name. Bob took Rex back to his car, they shook hands, and Rex went off to deal with the Westside Inn.

After his experience at the Lanier, he didn't know what to expect, but Jerry Thompson restored his faith in hotel people. The Westside Inn was nothing sensational, but it had a pleasant atmosphere and a cooperative staff. The conference room Jerry showed him was going to be sufficient, and the hotel dining staff would be pleased to arrange lunch in the adjoining room as often as required.

Jerry agreed to set aside a block of rooms for the students during the time needed, and he waved aside the offer of Rex's personal credit card.

"You are going to be around here for a long time and so am I," he said. "We will work these things out together."

They shook hands, and Rex headed back to the bank.

Hilary did not really understand what GNU was all about because she had been working primarily with manufacturing companies. Warehouses full of inventory or products served as proper collateral. Service organizations had no assets other than some office machines.

"It's hard to explain to the loan committee about the absence of hard assets," she explained. "They like to know that there is a chance of getting the money back."

"We're not asking for a loan yet," said Rex. "Anyhow, what kind of hard assets does a bank have? Do you have any warehouses full of inventory here? Banks are service organizations that make money by performing. We are the same, actually. We will have products because our seminars will be repeatable and will have standard material going along with them. All I need is a line of credit of about $50,000 to help with the ups and downs. I will be glad to offer my house as security. It's real."

Hilary nodded and smiled at him. "We won't need a house for a line of credit this size, Mr. Diamond. We want to help new businesses get started in the community, and we would appreciate it if you did your banking business here. We have a lot of services, including one that does payroll. It might interest you."

Rex sat up. He was very interested. "Does it do withholding and W-2s and all those mysterious things?"

"Absolutely. It was developed to help small businesses in particular, but it can handle any number of employees. If you will have your accountant call me; I'll be glad to lay out some start-up procedures."

Rex thought about that. "We don't have an accountant. Do you know anyone we could consider? I doubt whether we will need to employ a full-time accountant yet, but we might have to in the near future."

"You might want to hire an accounting firm to do the record keeping and bill paying for you on a fee basis. When you think your company has grown enough to afford its own accountant, then we will help you find one, if you wish.

"You also might want to consider having the results audited each year. That would have to be done by a firm other than the one that was helping you with the office work."

Rex nodded. "I understand that part, but I could use a firm now. Do you have any recommendations?"

"There are several in the area. Let me give you the names of two that the bank uses. One is a regional firm, and the other is an independent CPA. He's good, but he insists on working on his own. He's very fussy about taking on new clients. Hampton Cloth is his name. Here is a card on the other firm."

After bidding Hilary goodbye, Rex went back to his den to collapse. It was becoming apparent that his job consisted of positioning GNU in the community as well as with clients and with its own employees.

"What people think of you has a lot to do with the amount of success you will have," he thought.

The business of having a charter, a purpose, and clear requirements was becoming real to him. Those people today had taken him seriously, although he had very little money, no business, and no facilities. If he could make it all come out the way it sounded at lunch, then things would be very interesting indeed.

* * * *

THE ECOLOGICAL EXECUTIVE

Several years later, Rex brought the story up to date in his own words.

"I decided to write some thoughts about where we are in order to record what I have learned from my experience in bringing a new company on line. GNU started 3 years ago. Today we have 50 employees, 15 clients, 231 suppliers, 16 worthy causes we support, and offices in 2 buildings.

"Sales are $7.5 million, which is $150,000 per employee, and profit is 9 percent after tax, which amounts to $675,000. We owe the bank $143,234 on our credit line, and we have $350,000 in a CD. We are still fragile, but we have a solid base. With monthly compensation of under $200,000, including pension accrual, we would be able to ride out a short down turn.

"We have a medical insurance plan and are establishing an ESOP and a stock option program. The ESOP price was set by a firm that came in for 2 weeks and then multiplied the earnings per share by 3.

"All the present employees have stock which we sold then at 10 cents a share and lent them the money to buy. The professionals who joined us each have about 2 percent of the company, and others have proportionate shares. They don't care what the stock is worth. It just means a great deal to them to be participants, but some day it should be valuable. I own 40 percent; my family has 30 percent; and the rest belongs to the employees.

"I thought I would never get done with all the administrative things involved in setting up a company. Dealing with insurance people, banks, landlords, lawyers, attorneys, accountants—it goes on and on. As a result of this, we set up an administrative department headed by Joe Williams. He runs all the "nonprofessional" activities, including human resources, purchasing, and facilities. There are fifteen employees in those areas.

"The professional side of the house is managed by Wally Thompson, who does the seminars and consulting. Wally is a dedicated person who works very hard. He is also difficult to get along with now and then, but he does a good job.

"I developed the material for our course, and all twelve of the consultant-teachers have learned how to teach it. We have a notebook for the students and are conducting four or five classes each week. About 40 full weeks are available every year after holidays and such are deducted. The rest of our revenues come from on-site consulting and workshops.

"We still don't advertise, but we do make every effort to get our name in the articles written about purchasing improvements. I have been working on a book which should help, but the best source of new clients is still the third-person credibility supplied by satisfied clients. We have done a good job for them, and I am continually receiving letters from executives and managers who have attended our seminars, complimenting the GNU employees.

"That is really what these thoughts are about. I included information on the company just to show that we are successful to date and that we are organized. A lot of companies are equally well off.

"I wanted to set down what I have learned about management in terms of what I call the 'ecology of the company.' I think of it in terms of forest management. There are so many things involved in the life of a forest: the trees, plants, and other flora; the lakes and streams; the animals and their habits; the effects of outside forces. We still don't know how to avoid ruining a forest in our attempts at managing it.

"A company has the same problem. The employees all have life cycles and pressures. A secretary trying to get planned work done must deal with pressures from boss, customer, supplier, coworker, management, home, social life, and a dozen other sources.

"A squirrel trying to put food away for the winter must be concerned about predators, other squirrels, the weather, the nut supply, and a dozen other things. When human beings come along to harvest trees or build roads, it complicates things to the point of frustration.

"The head of an organization sets its tone, and I soon began to realize that this was so, even though I had heard it for years without understanding it. When we hired our first secretary, she came in to see me after 2 weeks to recommend a friend for the job that was going to be open soon. Then she asked me, 'Are we going to have holidays?'

"The thought had never occurred to me. In trying to produce a cash flow, I had learned to hate the weekends when we couldn't have classes or go see clients. I think I blushed.

" 'Gee, I guess so, Joyce. Come to think of it, we never got around to saying anything about it. What brought that up?'

" 'Today is Labor Day. I found out when I tried to call the bank.'

" 'OK,' I said. 'How about making up a list of the holidays you had where you used to work, and we'll ask everyone about it at the Family Council meeting on Friday. Usually there are about ten a year, I think.' Some time later, when I reminded her of that meeting and teased her about it, she commented that she would never have thought of going to see her previous boss about anything. He would not have appreciated it. I realized that she was being open because I was being open. That came about because I really didn't know what to do about many things and was looking for help.

"From that incident I learned to formalize my 'touring.' I would schedule at least 1 hour a day to walk around and chat with people. This provides an opportunity for just plain greeting (and sometimes hugging) people while taking their 'temperature' about status. Seeing concern on a previously smiling face is a definite indication that something is amiss.

"There are unspoken rules for the leader to obey when touring. First, 'Don't tell anyone to do anything.' A simple comment such as 'It is dark in here and we need some more ceiling light' is all it takes for someone to call a contractor and have the place torn up.

"Second, 'Don't criticize anything.' If something needs to be taken care of, do it through the proper organizational channels. (I must admit that I break this rule when it comes to housekeeping. At one time I had a special plaque made for one area that continually looked messy. This was the 'Collier Brothers Award,' named after two legendary brothers who lived in a mansion packed with earnestly retrieved old newspapers and other carefully packaged trash.)

"Third, 'Always be smiling and happy.' Employees look closely at the leader, very closely. It is not always easy to appear as if everything is great when real problems are sitting on the leader's shoulders, but it is necessary.

"Fourth, 'Don't miss anyone.' Some folks won't be around when the tour is made, but ask about them anyway.

"Fifth, 'Remember what they said.' On the next tour comment on things that came up during the last one. Employees can spot genuine interest or the lack of it from 50 yards away.

"It is from these tours that I learn what is really going on in this company. It was the same during my Lightblue days. Sitting in the headquarters office reading reports was delusion incorporated. It was only by going out to the facilities and touching that a glimmer of the truth would come forward. It didn't take long for the units to learn that they could level with me and not have it come roaring back to drown them.

"Touring can be learned.

"If forest managers could converse directly with the flora and fauna, they would make fewer mistakes. As it is, they have to learn through measurement, past experience, and research. Who thought, for instance, that an enormous body of water like Lake Erie could be put to sleep by overfertilization and industrial waste? Who would have thought it could have been brought back to life by eliminating those influences? But it has.

"When a company on the verge of disaster magically turns around and recovers, credit is usually given to financial restructuring. However, reality may tell a different story.

"The company changes because the 'spirit' changes. People start working again. They had become discouraged and downtrodden because of the feeling that the company was dying and the management was doing nothing about it. If the organization is large enough to be written about in the papers, they find the corporate name is always preceded by the words 'financially troubled.' It is hard to take.

"When a management team offers hope and positive leadership, the people start making things move again. Now, admittedly, if the product is obsolete, like buggy whips, then the company may never turn around. But in most cases it is just necessary to slice out the excessive overhead, get financial restructuring, and help people go to work. They will make the new management look great enough to get rich.

"Keeping the company from going to sleep, keeping the management team challenged and filled with dreams, offering the customers new and improved products, and creating an environment in which people enjoy hard work—this is what makes a company continually successful.

"It is 98 percent attitude, and attitude can be generated, assuming that the people involved are not terminally negative. Take the last Family Council.

> Rex: "Welcome to the thirty-sixth GNU Family Council. Today happens to be our third birthday. I understand that we are going to have a cake in the lounge after the meeting. [Applause.] Let me ask Joyce to open the meeting by returning thanks."
>
> Joyce: "Let us pray. Dear Lord, we thank you for your loving kindness and the attention you give our company. We thank you for your healing hand on Kenneth's daughter, Debbie, and we ask you to bless our communication today. Amen."
>
> Rex: "And now our financial wizard, Elizabeth Bronson."

CONTROLLER: "Thank you, Rex. We have good news and some not so good news this month. Let me put this overhead on the screen. As you can see, July was a good month in that we took in $781,000 and had expenses of $585,000. That gives us a $10 million running rate, which would fit in with our projections of a 35 percent growth this year. Expenses have held their own, and we are going to be at an annual rate of $154,000 sales per employee, even with the new hires coming aboard.

"The not so good news is that the backlog has fallen 10 percent and is actually below forecast. We are going to have to look into the cause of that.

"The board has approved the first deposit into the ESOP program, so we will be transferring $50,000 into that account next month. Any questions?"

HELEN: "I don't really understand ESOP. I know it means that we will have stock in the company, but how does it work?"

ELIZABETH: "It means Employee Stock Ownership Plan, and it's complicated. We have a pamphlet on it that will be sent out tomorrow [looks to the administrative assistant, who nods], but I am planning on bringing the administrator in at the next Family Council meeting to explain it to us. Roughly, it means that the company's contribution buys so much stock or other investments for you, and it belongs to you depending on the length of time you have been with the company. The time is called 'vesting,' and it takes 5 years to own the stock outright. When you retire or leave, it's yours. In the meantime, it can be counted as an asset for your personal balance sheet."

WALLY: "What's a balance sheet?" [Laughter.]

ELIZABETH: "Any other questions? If not, I will turn the lectern over to Human Resources. Joe?"

JOE: "Thank you, Elizabeth. As you can see from the overhead, we have fifty-one full-time employees, four on job sharing, and two temporaries. There are six openings approved by the Executive Committee, and they have been posted in the Human Resources area right outside Helen's office. If you are interested in any of those jobs, let us know. I will discuss the qualifications and such with you and then arrange interviews. Training is provided for five of them. One is for an MIS (management information system) specialist, and we might not have anyone here at this moment who will be able to step right into the job."

GEORGE: "Are we going to get into computers more?"

JOE: "Well, as you know, we already have a central processor that does the financial and personnel material. The thought is to see whether we can learn how to have a 'paperless office.' The study done last month by the Secretaries' Task Team showed that we don't use paper very well. You have all received copies of it, which generated more paper [laughter], but it shows a clear pattern. One thing that sticks in my mind is that 70 percent of all the copies made wind up in a desk or file. With a computer system, we could have it available on a disk and eliminate all that material.

"There will be a letter-writing clinic next Thursday, held in three different sessions so that everyone can attend. After the clinic those who want to get deeper into writing letters and reports will be offered the opportunity to attend after-work classes held in one of our classrooms.

"The new medical insurance brochure is now available in Human Resources. We will be sending them out next week, but if you need one sooner, call Helen or me. We are doing a study of how we use this insurance to see whether we can switch some of it around so that we can have better coverage with less expense. The average age in the company is 32, so we should be able to do better."

REX: "Thank you. Wally?"

WALLY: "The seminars are fully scheduled for the next 2 months, and there are six proposals outstanding, other than the ones we have that are being implemented. Some of these have taken a while to reach this stage. I think that's why the backlog has dropped, Elizabeth. But we will check it out and let you know for sure.

"We have time today to discuss some of what is happening in specific areas. I have asked Arthur to say a few words about a long-time client—Anson; Bill to talk about a new client—City Motors; and Herman to bring us up to date on a potential client—and this is a big one—International Bank. Arthur?"

ARTHUR: "Anson was the first client Mr. Diamond had, and it's been a good one. I spent 2 days at Anson last week. Sam Ellison took early retirement last year, as you know, and Everett Smith took over. The company has sent all its Purchasing people through our classes and is using the video material to bring the rest of its management up to date. The interesting thing is that departments all over the company, not just Purchasing, are using these principles for improvement. Everett is inviting them to school. Also, he told the Anson board that our services to date have cost the company $475,000, and it has documented audited savings of over $35 million. This doesn't count the interest cost saved through inventory elimination. That will be several million on its own. Anson is willing to talk to any company wanting a reference, and that is the end of my tale. I guess Bill is next, thank you." [Applause.]

BILL: "That's a hard act to follow, Arthur. City Motors is a misnamed company. It has operations all over the world, and it buys from suppliers all over the world. The company spends over $9 billion a year, about half of it in the United States. Most of its production is in the forty-eight contiguous states, but it also has plants in Europe and Africa.

"City Motors would like us to set its managers up with their own seminars, which we would write and then teach them to teach. The company would give us a royalty.

"The key Purchasing executives are coming to class here next week. Mr. Diamond is going to meet with them and perhaps play golf after the classes are over. They are really fired up. We would have to translate some of our videotapes and notebooks into several languages for them, but City Motors would pay for it.

REX: "Thanks. Herman is next." [Applause]

HERMAN: "International Bank would be an unusual client. The company mainly buys services like software and communication systems. But it also has long-range deals for paper, furniture, and other materials which it uses itself.

"Members of its management team came to us after hearing a speech that Wally made to an association last spring. They have been arguing about how a manufacturing consultant could help them.

"We will be finalizing a strategy as soon as they finish class. It's hard to talk to people who don't understand the principles of purchasing the way we do. But they are sincere, and we will have a good relationship with International Bank. Thank you." [Applause.]

WALLY: "Before we close this part of the meeting, I would like to introduce two new members of the Operations Department. A new management trainee, Gail Masters. Stand up Gail. [Applause.] Gail just graduated from MBA school last month. Welcome.

"A new writer for the Development Department, Keith Wright. Keith worked for Philadelphia newspapers before coming here. [Applause.]

"That's the end of the Operations report. [Applause.] Next is Development. Kermit?"

KERMIT: "We have some exciting things going. We are shooting videos of some of the cases we use in class. You may have seen some of it going on. We have been using actors from the city theater. It will be several weeks before the whole shoot is finished.

"That's what we Hollywood types call 'a shoot.' [Laughter.] But we have prevailed on them to release one clip so that you can see what's happening. Can we run that now?

[Room darkens and video lights up to show a 5-minute clip.]

"Also, we are working on a new company brochure. According to the old one, there are only about a dozen people in the corporation. Someone will be wandering around next week taking photos. One of us will be along so that you will know who is legitimate. If a photo of one of us looks good for the brochure, we will ask permission to use it first. That's all for Development. Carol is next." [Applause.]

CAROL: "I have a report from the Recreation Committee. The annual outing is scheduled for the 29th of next month at Edison Park. The whole family of the whole family is invited. There will be a nursery like last year, and free everything. Can I have a show of hands for anyone who will not, repeat, not be able to make it? Thank you, only a couple. We will ask everyone to sign up so that we can make plans. Don't miss it." [Applause.]

BUD: "I am supposed to report on the status of the Quality Improvement Team. We have sent out problem request forms to everyone and will be asking for them back in 2 weeks. These will let us get help for you if something is not being fixed. You only need to know the problem, not the answer. Also, our second annual Zero Defects Day will be coming up in the next couple of months. To keep up the suspense, we are not saying exactly what is going to happen. Thank you." [Applause.]

REX: "This has been a stimulating meeting. Now let's have an open discussion. We can talk about anything that anyone wants to talk about. Nancy?"

NANCY: "Mr. Diamond, I've been wondering about how big the company is going to get. What do you think we will see in the next few years?"

REX: "Well, Nancy, I'm not sure I'm the one to ask. I kept saying we would never be more than twenty-five people, and we are double that. My guess is that we will continue to grow at a 30 percent rate for the next 5 years and then at a slower rate. How many is that, Elizabeth?"

ELIZABETH: "At 30 percent, we would double every 2.4 years. In

5 years we would have 200 people." [Laughter; burst of applause.]

REX: "If that's going to be so, then we will have to learn how to manage a firm of that size. We are planning an off-site strategy session between now and the next Family Council. I will give a full report on these results, if any, at the next meeting. What else should we talk about?"

CHARLIE: "We are having a hard time getting the mail all around the building twice a day. Do you think we could set up mail pickup stations? Each department could come to its station and get the mail. Bringing it around to each desk is what takes up all the time."

REX: "What is the consensus on that?"

HELEN: "We wouldn't get to see Charlie every day." [Laughter.]

SALLY: "It would mean a lot more running around, and we might miss something."

REX: "Joe, would you get Charlie and a couple of department secretaries together to chat about this? Anyone want to be in on the discussion? OK. You have them, Joe? Let us know when you make up your mind. In the meantime, Charlie, you can toss my mail in the lake. It just keeps me chained to the desk. Who else?"

ARTHUR: "I think we are going to have a capacity problem soon. Right now, we are really full for the next few months. Have we thought about setting up an operation on the West Coast?"

REX: "It has been discussed. I guess I never felt there was a need out there, but I am willing to take another look. Let's make that part of the strategy meeting, Joe. If we have to grow that way, I would like to do as much of the work as possible right here. [Cheers.]

"Time's up. Charolette is going to close the meeting."

CHAROLETTE: "Thank you. I wanted to share a reading with everyone. This is called "The Station." It's by Robert Hastings."

Tucked away in our subconscious is an idyllic vision. We see ourselves on a long trip that spans the continent. We are traveling by train. Out the windows we drink in the passing scene of cars on nearby highways, of children waving at a crossing, of cattle grazing on a distant hillside, of smoke pouring from a power plant, of row upon row of corn and wheat, of flatlands and valleys, of mountains and rolling hillsides, of city skylines and village halls.

But uppermost in our minds is the final destination. On a

certain day at a certain hour we will pull into the station. Bands will be playing and flags waving. Once we get there so many wonderful dreams will come true and the pieces of our lives will fit together like a completed jigsaw puzzle. How restlessly we pace the aisles, damning the minutes for loitering—waiting, waiting, waiting for the station.

"When we reach the station, that will be it!" we cry. "When I'm 18." "When I buy a new 450 SL Mercedes Benz!" "When I put the last kid through college." "When I have paid off the mortgage!" "When I get a promotion." "When I reach the age of retirement, I shall live happily ever after!"

Sooner or later we must realize there is no station, no one place to arrive at once and for all. The true joy of life is the trip. The station is only a dream. It constantly outdistances us.

"Relish the moment" is a good motto, especially when coupled with Psalm 118:24: "This is the day which the Lord hath made; we will rejoice and be glad in it." It isn't the burdens of today that drive men mad. It is the regrets over yesterday and the fear of tomorrow. Regret and fear are twin thieves who rob us of today.

So stop pacing the aisles and counting the miles. Instead, climb more mountains, eat more ice cream, go barefoot more often, swim more rivers, watch more sunsets, laugh more, cry less. Life must be lived as we go along. The station will come soon enough.

REX: "That's it. Have a great weekend."

Thus ended a typical Family Council gathering.

THROUGH THE KNOTHOLE AT GNU

"As part of the executive education we offer, I had arranged for John Mallory to visit us each week and have a general discussion with the students. John is recognized as an authentic authority on writing business letters and on the whole field of business communication. He can help people realize that writing is just conversing in a different form.

"John had agreed to help out for a few sessions but has shown up every week. The board authorized him to purchase a few shares of stock, and he bought it feeling that he was helping us out. I am pleased to see that it is now worth something.

"As we were walking to lunch last month, he asked me how long I thought we would continue to grow so dramatically.

" 'I am always a pessimist, as you know,' John said. 'But I would think that you will start to see a slowdown, and one of these days there will be some competition.'

"I shook my head. 'We would welcome some competition,' I said. 'We think we could stay ahead of everyone, and having competitors would let everyone know how really good we are. Also, it would keep us from becoming complacent.'

" 'Then you think the growth will go on forever?'

" 'That's a long, long time. But I do feel that we are getting more and bigger clients. Look at City Motors and International Bank. Between them they have several hundred thousand employees. More companies will come along later.'

" 'That's good to hear.'

"What John was saying made me a little uneasy, so I dropped by Elizabeth's office on the way back. She was peering into her computer.

" 'What do you find so interesting in there, Beth?' I asked. 'I always have the feeling that you bean counters live in a different world than the rest of us.'

"She smiled. 'Who is to say which is the real world? I was just checking up on the backlog.'

" 'You said at Family Council that it had dropped off 10 percent. I assumed that was just a normal fluctuation. Is there a trend developing?'

" 'Yes, I think so. From what I can determine, our older clients like Anson are dropping off. They aren't making as many bookings as before. The newer ones like City Motors haven't started yet.'

" 'Are we looking at a blank spot in our tape? Do you see a gap between what we have scheduled and what is going to happen?'

" 'I think we should ask Operations, but it sure looks that way.'

" 'If we had a period of, say, 3 months in which we had a gap before the new clients started to take effect, how bad would it be for us financially?'

" 'It could be devastating. We have a reserve of about $200,000. That would handle the payroll for 1 month. We have a line of credit that we could borrow against.'

" 'But even a worst-case falloff wouldn't be total. We would still have some money coming in. If we saw a drop of 50 percent, which would be high, for a few months, that would give us revenue of about $400,000 against our current expenses of $585,000. That's a deficit of $185,000. And if we cut things back a little, we could have a shortfall of around $100,000 a month. If we had a 5-month problem, we would be in the hole for half a million dollars.'

"Beth smiled and nodded in agreement. "I would think that would be about right. With our reserve of $200,000 and a $300,000 loan from the bank we could handle the cash-flow problem. However, there is another kicker involved.'

" 'Kicker?'

" 'Yes, the new employee education system.'

" 'Oh my,' I said. 'That slipped my mind. We are planning to spend $600,000 over the next 6 months to produce it. If we had it now, we wouldn't be having this problem. Anson would be buying enough to offset any downswing.'

" 'So we have a million-dollar problem?'

" 'Looks like it. I think the bank will help some; I could go talk to them.'

" 'Let's get the Executive Committee together first. We are going to need a plan before we hit the bank. And I would like to make certain that the guesses we are making are in the ballpark. Unfortunately, I have the feeling that we are right on target.'

"The Executive Committee gathered by 3 P.M. Beth and I presented what we saw as the problem, and I asked for comments.

" 'I think there is a little too much gloom spreading here,' said Wally. 'We can pump up sales a little during this period, slow down on the new product, cut back on the employees, and coast through it.'

"Kermit didn't think that was such a good idea. 'We can't "slow down" on a big project like the employee education system. We are using a lot of studio time; we have commitments to a dozen actors; we have to schedule the printers and binders for the books. Also, we have told clients that it would be ready in 6 months, and they are going to count on it. I think that's the big reason that International Bank and City Motors are coming with us.'

" 'If we cut back on employees, we will be damaging morale quite a bit,' said Joe. 'We just recruited a few folks; if we lay them off right away, it will look like we don't know what we are doing.'

"Beth sighed. 'We are going to have to cut 20 percent out of the payroll anyway just to get in line with our survival plan. Something will have to be done. We can't go to the bank for a million dollars without having a plan that shows we're taking a little pain.'

"Wally stood up and went to the board. 'OK,' he said. 'Let's brainstorm a little. What can we cut out that will let us tighten our cash flow? I'll put down 'fly tourist' first. That should save us $35,000 a year.'

" 'How about employee birthday dinners?'

" 'We can eliminate office material inventory and order as needed.'

" 'Let's cancel the leases on the duplicating equipment.'

" 'Can we get our landlords to lower the rents for a period?'

" 'Ask the suppliers to not bill us for their margins until the crisis is over.'

" 'We could all take a 20 percent cut in pay.'

" 'How about putting everyone on a 4-day week instead?'

" 'We could postpone the ESOP payment and stall the pension fund until the end of the year.'

" 'We can stop all purchasing as of right now and look at each case on an individual basis.'

" 'No new hiring.'

" 'Cut out the picnic.'

"After 15 minutes Wally had both boards covered.

" 'There are a lot of things we can do,' said Wally. 'We don't have to be depressed about it. We may have found the problem early enough to fix it.'

" 'OK,' I said. 'Now all of this is no one's fault. If any blame is to be assigned, it should come to me. As Wally says, we caught the problem early enough and we need to move out on it. First, we will spend no money at all for anything unless this team approves of it in advance. We will take no trips at all unless they are revenue trips, but we don't do much of that anyway. Also, we will fly tourist, not because it saves money so much but because it will remind people of our situation.

" 'This team will meet in my office every morning at eight for a few moments. I want each of you to sit with your staff and figure out how to cut the expenses of your operation 30 percent for the next 6 months. After that time we should be able to recover.'

" 'I am going to ask the associates to work a 4-day week for the duration of this emergency. We will make it up to them when we get well.'

" 'Joe, I would like to have a special Family Council Friday afternoon. In the meantime, Beth and I will go talk to the bank. Wally, how about you and your senior people preparing a special presentation for the bank executives. I will invite them to come over later this week.'

"Wally nodded in agreement. "Perhaps it might be a good idea to have Kermit show some of the new product.'

" 'Good idea. Now let's close with prayer.'

"Beth and I walked into Bob Wilson's office just as Hilary Swat arrived. We were greeted warmly and introduced to Alex Drum, whom I had not met before.

" 'Alex has had a lot of experience working with some of our small-business clients,' said Bob. 'I thought he might be able to be of some assistance in your case.'

"Alex nodded pleasantly.

" 'Good. Beth and I will bring you up to date with our status, and then we would like to invite all of you over to GNU later this week so that you can see more of what we are doing.'

" 'First, let me point out that our revenues this year will be about 50 percent over last year. We project the same amount of growth for next year. Our revenues per employee are approaching $154,000, which is a remarkable figure in an economy where the average is well below $75,000.'

" 'We find ourselves in a cash-flow bind that is compounded

by the development costs of a new product. We feel that we will have an operating problem over the next 4 months of $100,000 a month. That's after reducing our expenses quite a bit. The EES (employee education system) will cost us $600,000 over the next 6 months. We could stretch it out a little, but that would raise the cost.'

" 'Beth sent you our latest financial statement, including operating costs. So what we would like to arrange with you is a million-dollar line of credit to get us through this period. I think the projections we have will more than cover that amount of money.'

"Bob nodded in agreement, and Alex smiled.

" 'You marketing types are always overoptimistic,' he said. 'I would want to take a closer look before agreeing to such a large sum.'

"I bristled. 'I am not sure what you mean by "marketing type," ' I said. 'But I assure you that our figures are very conservative and sound. GNU is a well-managed company.'

" 'I am sure it is, Rex,' said Alex. 'But there are always things lying around that management is too close to see. Look at travel, for instance. You could cut that way back; it's almost $50,000 every month.'

" 'But we don't make a trip unless it's for revenue. That's the way we make half our money. We are a consulting company.'

" 'I am sure each trip has a purpose and meaning, but they can't all make money.'

"I gasped. Beth leaned forward.

" 'When one of our consultants goes somewhere, we bill the client $2000 a day. A consultant's trip must be at least two days. So the client pays for all expenses, and we take the rest as revenue. We have fewer than 10 trips a year that aren't conducted that way, and those are to go to professional meetings.'

" 'It would seem to me that if you have managed without this new product this long you could postpone it until next year. According to your projections, you could be out of this problem in a few months if you stopped the product.'

" 'That's a fair point,' I said. 'What we see is that our biggest new clients are coming with us because they see this product as the way to educate their entire corporations. They might hold it all back otherwise.'

"Bob stirred. 'What sort of additional security could we count on, Rex? Our board hasn't had much experience with consulting companies, and the members will be nervous. You know how boards are.'

" 'How much of the million dollars will they be nervous about?' I asked.

" 'I would suspect about two-thirds of it, certainly half.'

"Beth spoke up. 'Our office equipment, including the new computer, which we own, is on the balance sheet for $400,000. Accounts receivable at present are $1,450,000, and we could pledge them. I think that would be enough. All our clients pay on time and are as blue-chip as one can get.'

" 'Accounts receivable for an intangible are easy to walk away from,' said Alex.

" 'Alex,' I noted, 'I was introduced to you with the under-standing that you were going to be of help to us. So far you have acted more like an undertaker than a helper. I would not want you to be talking to our people in this manner if you come over to the operation later this week.'

"There was an embarrassed silence. Then Bob cleared his throat. 'We want to help you, Rex and Beth. Our bank has faith in your company, and we have appreciated your business over the years. Your request is completely in line, but we are going to be asked some difficult questions by the Loan Committee. We have to make certain we understand.'

"Alex nodded. 'I don't mean to be negative, Rex, and I am sorry if I come across that way. I know how much this company must mean to you. I just have to get the facts, as they used to say on *Dragnet*. Most of my experience has been with manufac-turing companies. If you all will be patient with me, I'll do my best to learn your business.'

" 'OK,' I said. 'Now as for security, I would be willing to put up my house here in town plus my vacation home. I think the equity in them totals about $350,000. Of course, you could get an appraisal.'

" 'That won't be necessary,' said Bob. 'We don't need any

more expenses right now. Beth, can you and Hilary sit down and get all these numbers together?'

" 'We will authorize the $400,000 line of credit at $100,000 a month beginning right now. I'll have to take the other $600,000 to the board next week. Perhaps we could arrange the presentation you mentioned for Thursday? I could bring along two board members.'

" 'That will be fine. What time would be best for you?' I asked.

" 'After 4 P.M. Banker's hours, you know.'

" 'We will see you then. Beth, I'll walk on back. See you at the office.'

"I was furious inside, partly because of the attitude I had been faced with and partly because I had let myself get into this situation.

"All during my career, I had lived with the phrase, 'Never run out of cash.' It was part of the living experience—but it was only a phrase in a big corporation. There, the criterion was bookkeeping.

"If an operation overspent and came out negative in the cash flow, the general manager got a lecture; if it happened again, the manager even got fired. But the lack of cash was made up by a paper transfer within the company.

"Here, Beth and I were without enough actual real money to make the payroll next month. This month we could cash in a CD. Next month somebody was not going to get paid if we didn't get the transfusion. It would take a little while to stop spending—a lot of things were committed.

"We had to buy lunches for the students. Each week there were about 100 lunches at $6 or so apiece. That would pay the salaries of three of our classroom setup people. Suddenly money had a totally different look.

"That afternoon we returned to the bank and signed over our properties as security. The bank's attorney had an inch-thick pile of material for Caroline and me to sign. She never blinked, but I was not too gracious about it. It was apparent to me that these people didn't think we were going to make it.

"I considered going to another bank but decided they would

all be the same, and the others would know even less about us. If we got out of this bind—*when* we got out of this bind—I would spend more time letting the community know what we were all about. By the time I finished, they would want to pour money into us.

"But we were never going to run out of cash again. Scout's honor.

"Wally, Kermit, and Arthur took the bank people through our operation in a masterful way. I deliberately stayed out of the presentation so that the bank people could understand that we had a competent staff.

"There could be no doubt after it was all over that we knew what we were doing.

"Beth presented the financial status, and even Alex had to be impressed that we knew enough about our cash flow to recognize we were in trouble before most companies would have noticed.

"We arranged that Beth and I would meet on a weekly basis with Alex and Hilary. We would also keep them informed about any changes. We were set for the next 6 weeks anyway.

"True to our predictions, student enrollment fell during the following period, dragging revenues along with it. We were on plan that far anyway.

"At the special Family Council, I had laid out the situation for all the associates to see. They had agreed to cut back to a 4-day week, but most were still working 5 days anyway. I discovered that Caroline had contacted some of the lower-level people and was assisting them financially so that they would not suffer too much.

"As the end of the second month approached, it was becoming apparent to both Beth and me that the payroll was going to be sticky. I was not taking any salary at all, but that didn't help a great deal. We were going to need $25,000 more than the promised $100,000 to make our other expenses and the payroll too.

"I had been invited to speak to the top 250 executives of City Motors, who were having a conference in Palm Springs. Beth agreed to go tell the bank of our need, and I flew out to Los Angeles and back to Palm Springs. The dinner that evening was a fine opportunity to meet the chairperson and other senior executives of City. They were very enthusiastic about our relationship and were looking forward to my keynote remarks the next morning.

"At six o'clock the next morning my telephone rang. It was Beth.

" 'I hate to disturb you at this hour—I know it's the middle of the night out there—but Alex insisted he had to talk to you. Here he is.'

" 'Rex? Alex. I am very concerned that we have this enormous problem here and you are in Palm Springs. I think you should come back immediately so that we can get to work on it.'

" 'Alex,' I muttered, 'do you realize that I am out here—and getting paid for it—to speak to the top management of our biggest customer? Do you realize that our future depends on how well I speak in about 2 hours? And what is so enormous about $25,000?'

" 'It just doesn't look right for you to be out there when there is so much trouble back here.'

" 'Do you want me to tell City Motors to arrange for an hour's worth of organ music so that I can go back and hold your hand? Well, it's impossible. Beth can handle anything you want, and I will be flying back tonight on the red-eye. Come see me at 9 A.M. tomorrow.'

" 'I am going to have to tell the board about this.'

" 'Alex, you are a dimwit!' I hung up.

"There is something solid about knowing you are at the end of your rope. It makes one think. There I was, frustrated in my world crusade by a small-town bank that thought $25,000 was a lot of money.

"There was no way to change the bank's attitude, so I needed another way to handle the situation. Why should big companies be able to survive the bumps in the road, while little companies have to be successful every moment? I really laid it into the City executives in my speech. After it was all over there could be no doubt in anyone's mind that City had a great opportunity and that the people in that room were the keys to taking advantage of it.

"Harold Green, the chairman, asked me whether I could join him, the chief financial officer, and a board member for golf after lunch. I hadn't brought my clubs, but I figured I could do as well with a stick since I hadn't played for 2 years. In my present state of mind I was not too particular, so I rented a set, bought yet another pair of golf shoes and a sweater, and joined them.

"It was a delightful experience. I realized that over the past few weeks I had forgotten how to enjoy myself. In the grill room we got around to discussing business.

" 'You have a great operation, Rex,' said Harold. 'I admire you for stepping out to start it up. You are going to make a big difference to this corporation, and from what we hear, you have already done that for Anson.'

" 'Thank you, sir,' I said. 'We are very proud of what Anson has done.'

"I paused and thought about it for a moment; then I decided to level with them.

" 'We are in a bit of a bind at the moment though. We are developing a new product at the same time as some clients are slowing down, such as Anson, and others are beginning, such as City.'

" 'So you have a cash-flow problem,' he stated.

" 'You got it.'

" 'That's what business is all about. I realize that big companies can always float a loan or some stock, but small operations are at the mercy of lending institutions.'

"I was startled. 'Have you been reading my mail?'

"The CFO laughed. 'We don't have to. It happens to every new company. You have probably been blaming yourself. But it's just a lack of capital for start-up. Growing out of the cash flow always catches up with you. That's the way most small businesses fail. GNU has had a great growth pattern, and it's a very well managed company. You will make it.'

"I blushed. 'I am not too certain about that. Right now we see a million-dollar deficit for the next 6 months. After that we will do well, but I am not certain the bank is going to let us live that long. At 6 A.M. I got a call that the bank people were getting nervous, and we have only drawn down $100,000 of our credit line.'

"Harold nodded. 'Banks don't understand service operations. They like us because we are a manufacturing company, but we make most of our money through our financial operation and car leasing. Banks like a warehouse full of castings. We keep one around just to show them. We would like to help you out, Rex. What would be the best way?'

"I was startled and couldn't think of anything to say at the moment. The CFO was doodling on his scorecard.

" 'Let me think out loud,' he said. 'We would need a "business reason" to do something. As I remember the strategy the team worked out, City was going to spend a lot of money with GNU over the next several years.'

" 'One way we could handle it is that we could pay you a retainer up front in return for a discount on the total. Another way is that we could take an equity position in GNU.'

"The chairman smiled. 'I would suspect that from your Lightblue experience you already know how undesirable it would be to have a corporation our size for a partner. But we would be proud to work something out.'

"I thought about it. 'If you could give us a retainer of $400,000, we could provide you with a discount that would let you save $100,000, over the next 18 months. Then if you could also cosign the $600,000 line of credit against an equity position, we would be in absolutely terrific shape.'

"I was getting excited. 'That would be wonderful. We would be willing to put someone from City on our board if that would provide a comfort factor. It would be of help to us to have that experience available.'

" 'We might consider that in the future. We are hoping that you and your company will have a long-term relationship with us, and we both want to be successful.'

"We made arrangements to handle the details of the transaction during the following week, and I called Beth to let her know the news. This arrangement would let us fight our own way out of our own problem, and everyone would benefit.

"But things seem to happen in bunches, as my grandmother used to say. The day I returned, I was called by the president of a new bank who wanted to take me to lunch. After a few polite comments he stated that his bank would like to finance our company. I told him we had a million-dollar problem, but he didn't even blink.

"Noticing my reaction, he chatted a little about his history. He had come here after working for 10 years in Manhattan, where low-level bank officers deal in million-dollar amounts. He liked what he knew about GNU and was willing to get into bed with us.

"I called the City CEO and asked his advice. He thought we should take the offered retainer from City and also establish the line of credit at the new bank.

" 'Stash the $400,000 away for emergencies,' he counseled. 'It would be somewhat complicated for us to cosign a note, although we would do it. Giving us a discount won't affect anything, particularly if it comes out of the EES material, which is all profit anyway.'

"I thanked him and followed his advice. Bob Wilson still gets nervous when we run into each other, but I am civil to him. Alex I ignore.

"We run the company differently now—from a financial control standpoint, that is. Everything else we do the same way.

"We pulled out of our tailspin after 6 months and were completely in the black again in 8 months. We had offered to pay the suppliers interest on what we owed them and did so. We drew down only $625,000 of the line of credit, and the $400,000 is still stashed away.

"We have a lot of assets now, but we still pretend we are almost broke. A public offering is planned as soon as we have 3 unscarred years. Going public is a lot of trouble, but it will provide the financial security we need to develop the products that will make us—and keep us—number one."

Chapter

Thoughts on Personnel Evaluation

Unfortunately not everyone is as sweet, cooperative, and effective as I am. Some folks are difficult to deal with. Probably all of us are difficult at some time or other, and that is a fact we have to accept.

"Smedley is a little abrupt and insensitive at times, but he is really a brilliant person."

"She gets a little yippy when the pressure comes on, but overall she has been very useful."

"He blows his top, but you just have to ride out the storm—it is all over in a few moments. Then he is really sorry about it, and we get back to work."

"Mrs. Johnson never says a good word about anyone, but she comes in every day and gets her stuff done."

Apparently there is a requirement that people are permitted, perhaps expected, to produce a little pain along with their product. Their contribution to the effort is one thing; their contrariness is another. It is possible to develop a contri-contra index.

If we have a salesperson who sells twice as much as anyone else, we might learn to forgive not receiving call reports each Monday morning. The doctor who produces one cure after another might be permitted a certain amount of crustiness and tyranny. The cook whose omelets float off the plate can get away with snarling at the boss.

At least for a while.

There is a ratio, which I am not about to attempt to measure by formula, of how much we are willing to put up with to accomplish something. If we really want to make a task happen, then we are willing to overlook the contra tendencies and practices of the individuals involved.

In fact, we may have learned to feel that a little pain is necessary if something is to be good. We know that anything which tastes good is bound to be bad for us and that the only way to keep our weight down is to suffer. Exercise has to hurt; we have to live on the edge of poverty in order to appreciate what we get later in life; and so on. All these myths may or may not be true; it depends on the individual.

But I have never understood why people who are supposed to be smart have to be rude or unfeeling in their relations with others. If they are so smart, they must understand that the way to gain cooperation is to have people think you are interested in them. Perhaps they are insecure or want to gain more attention. That is a problem for the psychologists to tackle.

Our interest is in how to deal with such people in a way that reduces the contra without hurting the contribution. It has to be done in a way that they understand. And it must be done with the assumption that they don't realize they are a perpetual pain in the tail.

People go through life without recognizing that what they put forth as a smile, others may read as a snarl. I gained a lifelong friend 35 years ago by pumping up my courage to tell a coworker that he had bad breath. He couldn't understand why people winced when he got close to them. He had been to a counselor and talked to his family. They wouldn't tell him. Every year I get a birthday card, a Christmas present, and several notes from him. He also has a very big job in the company that wouldn't make him an assistant supervisor back then. The experience encouraged me to be honest with people. You can tell anyone anything if it is done with love. Here is a transcript of a recent session I had.

"Come on in, Wally. It's good to see you."

"I have some of the lawyers coming in later this morning. If they had let me look at that lease before signing it, we could have saved a lot of trouble."

"What kind of trouble?"

"Well, it's for too long a period of time, and there's no option to buy the property if we ever want to do that. Anyway, I think I can save it."

"Have you talked with the facilities people about this? Do they know you are unhappy with the lease?"

"I asked one of them to come to the meeting this morning with the lawyers. You know them. They don't think ahead. I've tried to get through to them, but I guess I am going to have to take care of these things myself. You should have been more careful when you picked Joe Williams to head up that group. He really isn't too smart."

"How did you get involved with all this? It really isn't your area."

"I consider that my responsibility is to the company. I've put a lot of effort into this operation and hope that I've made at least a small contribution. But if we are going to grow right, we just have to take care of these details."

"I thought our primary job was to develop people. We can't do too much development if we interfere with their work."

"It takes a lot of time to develop people. If you want to let them run helter-skelter, then that's the way I'll do it. But these people should be watched, or they will get us into a lot of trouble."

"Does it occur to you that whenever we talk about something you are working on, it always turns into a confrontation instead of a discussion? I think we need to talk about that. How about sitting down?"

"Well, you keep questioning my motives. If I have to explain everything I am going to do, then I will never get anything done. I had a hard time getting that situation with the airplane straightened out last week. The one where we had to cancel the charter flight."

"Wally, the policy we have around here is that we don't charter airplanes. Right or wrong, that is the policy. You helped write the policy. Why did we ever charter the plane in the first place?"

"I had to make a judgment, and that was my decision. Believe me, it was embarrassing to have to back out and cancel. It cost us $500 at that."

"But you know that we don't go around policy. If a policy is wrong, we sit down and agree on a better one. You feel that you can change policies whenever you want. We have to get straight on that."

"I thought that executives were supposed to make decisions."

"They are. Decisions, I might add, that execute the will of the owners of the company, who are represented by the Executive Committee. How am I supposed to know what's happening around here if you make it up as you go along?"

"But I have a lot of experience."

"Wally, let's stop right here. I am getting tired of this constant quarreling. I don't think you realize how difficult you make it for yourself and for the rest of us by being so hard to deal with. There is no need for it. You have a great deal of experience. You are one of the smartest people I have ever known, and you are good at your job. But you sure are hard to handle."

"I don't see that."

"Let me finish. I invited you in for a friendly talk to get brought up to date on the status of your operation. Ever since you came in here, you have been berating me or others about something. You haven't said 'hello' or shaken my hand or even smiled. In a couple of minutes you have criticized the Executive Committee, a couple of employees, and by inference my management of the company. Would you like to spend time with someone who behaves like that?"

"I'm just trying to do my job. I have to call it the way I see it. That's just the way I am."

"Well, I'm not so sure you have to be that way. I think it might just be easier for you to beat up on people. Let me show you what I've been thinking about. I'll take this chart and draw a line on it to show your contribution to the company on a scale of 0 to 10. Unscientific, but my opinion. In the last 5 years you have gone from 8 to 9 to 7 to 6 to 6."

"That means that my effectiveness is falling? Why should that be? I am working night and day, and you said yourself that I know more about what's going on than anyone."

"I think the other line on the chart will show you the reason. It's also my opinion, but I think others would verify it. It's my contrary, or 'hard to get along with,' line. In those same 5 years you went from 3 to 4 to 7 to 8 to 9."

"You really think other people feel that way?"

"We can ask them if you wish. But be assured that the main reason I am going through all of this with you is that people are complaining. They all respect your contribution, but frankly, Wally, you are just getting to be too much trouble."

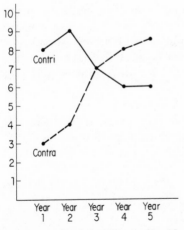

Figure 1   The Contri/Contra Considerations Chart.

"That's hard to believe. I always felt that the employees respected me. Tell me which ones are having the problem, and I'll go talk to them."

"Wally, I did that twice before, and you went out and intimidated them. You are just going to have to understand that it's your problem, not their problem. You are the one who is going to have to recognize it and do something about it."

"Would you like me to leave the company?"

"No, I would not like that. But we can't go along in this manner; it has to change. All I want you to do is accept that a change in your management style is in order. If you want respect, you have to show respect."

"I have always put the job first."

" 'Fight the job, not the people' is what the old man used to say. I think you are fighting the people."

"Can we talk about this some more as we go along? Maybe I do get a little carried away. What would you suggest I do about this lease business?"

"I would suggest that you hold off on the lawyers and have a private meeting with Joe in his office. Tell him you don't really understand the thought behind that particular lease and would appreciate being brought up to date. Then if you still don't agree, tell him your reasons. The items you cited seem pertinent to me, and I suspect he will agree. That way you are helping him out, not humiliating him in front of everyone."

"I'm beginning to see what you mean. Can I take this index chart with me? I'll stick it inside my desk drawer and plot myself."

"Be my guest."

"I appreciate your taking the interest in me to discuss this. It was good chatting with you this morning. See you later."

SENIOR EXECUTIVE PERFORMANCE EVALUATION FORMAT

Name of Senior Director _____

Responsibility _____

Name of evaluator _____

Responsibility _____

Execution of overall responsibility _____ A   B   C   D

*Contri*butions:

1. _____
2. _____
3. _____

*Contra*butions:

1. _____
2. _____
3. _____

Main strengths:

1. _____
2. _____

Main concerns:

1. _____
2. _____

Reviewee's comments:

_____   _____

Executive's Signature   Evaluator's Signature

Things You Need to Know Something About

One of the things I learned again after several years of running a company is that no one knows everything about everything. Sometimes I wonder if we really know anything at all for sure. As part of this thought process, I began to make a list of some items that I had to rethink or investigate during this time. Many of them are discussed in this chapter in terms that I hope reach the essence of the subject.

In any case, they are things we all should know something about if we are going to run something.

ABILITY

How do you know whether someone is capable of doing something? What are the key characteristics you should look for to know whether a person is the right one for the job? History abounds with stories of people who were underestimated. The ledger is balanced by tales of disasters caused by people who were overestimated. There are individuals who never did an honest day's work before they went out and conquered the enemies of their nations. There are others who became billionaires after being rejected by the ones who knew them best. Ability is not all that apparent unless you are willing to look for it.

To recognize ability, keep an open mind because it does not come in a specific package. But qualified people will have most of these characteristics:

- They will know who you are.
- They will have goals that make sense to you.
- They will not consider money in their first comments.
- They will ask questions in order to understand the tasks assigned.
- They will not require direction after that.
- They will complete their jobs properly on schedule.
- They will create work.
- They will be the same all the time.
- They will not make trouble unless it is necessary.
- They will be pleasant to all.

Ability means having the talent and energy to perform.

ABSENTEEISM

When people don't come to work, they are absent. Some people are absent even when they do come to work. There are two reasons for this: (1) some people just don't have consistent work habits; (2) the work they do is not appreciated, interesting, or both.

The management that tolerates people who do not show up for work sows the worst kind of seeds. People need permission to be absent, permission they receive from management's reaction to absenteeism. Managers give permission without realizing it. They don't check up on people. They don't have an interview on the subject after each incident. They grant sick days, giving the impression that employees are expected to take them. This encourages people to feel that they are not important.

To eliminate chronic absenteeism, the employer has to examine relations with employees, their work assignments, and the overall staffing. Organizations with too many employees suffer most from absenteeism. Gimmicks such as attendance prizes will not fix it. Selecting employees more carefully and expecting the best from them at work will set the proper tone. Those who love their work appear every day—anyway. Zero absenteeism should be expected.

ACCOUNTANTS

Those who practice accounting are called *accountants*. They use the rules of accounting to keep track of the money that goes through a business. These rules are not based on logic, and for the most part, the results of their application cannot be used for managing unless translated. Almost every company has its own Accounting Department which keeps ledgers and books on a current basis. This lets management know how much money is on hand, how much is owed to suppliers and banks, and how much is owed by customers. Constant items such as inventory, pension, and depreciation are also documented.

Every company needs to be audited regularly. The standard practice is to hire an outside accounting firm that provides auditors who pore over each piece of paper and determine whether what you think you have is what you really have. It is very important to do this because otherwise you will never know. The result of this effort is a financial statement. If you ever plan to have a public offering of stock, make certain that the auditing firm is one of the major, well-known companies. They don't do any better job, but they provide some credibility.

As with any other professional service, listen to what your accountants say, but do what you think best—it is your operation.

ADEPT

This acronym refers to a company statement to its employees on how they are supposed to act. It came about when I had made a comment that we should all be "professional." Someone with good sense asked me to be specific. The result was a set of requirements that we all put together and called ADEPT.

A is for Accurate. We all recognize that we have an obligation to do what we say we will do and to be precise in our reporting. If someone asks us what time it is, we should either respond with the correct time or say that we don't know but will find out.

D is for Discreet. We don't gossip about each other or the folks we do business with. We wear proper clothes. We act in an adult fashion. We are modest but not shy.

E is for Enthusiastic. We try to hire enthusiastic people and keep them enthusiastic. One cannot pretend enthusiasm for very long.

P is for Productive. We should each do our work completely and also lend a helping hand where necessary. The more employees we have, the less there is to share.

T is for Thrifty. We do everything first-class, but there is no need to throw money away. We must respect the company's funds as being separate from our own.

(Ask all employees to vote for the person who most fits each of these categories. Every quarter, have a committee choose one person for each category and award a desk plaque. This peer recognition is most appreciated.)

ADVERTISING

Advertising is a system of telling potential customers about your services or needs. All organizations advertise, whether they admit it or not. Charitable and community organizations don't do it as formally as businesses, but they find ways to get known.

Much of the lore of advertising is aimed at the clever phrase that gets people's attention. However, the most useful advertising for the majority of companies is the routine type. A regular notice in the same place all the time will help the customer find you when the customer is ready. Hardly anything beats the "yellow pages" type of advertising.

People are suspicious of slogans and displays that are so clever they appear insincere. The best advertising is third-person credibility—a customer telling a new or potential one about you. Give your customers a reason to do this.

The advertising budget for a charitable organization should be about 5 percent of receipts. It doesn't need to be that high if it can piggyback on the ads of others. Direct mail is the most useful if a sincere and personalized approach can be used. Remember that 80 percent of the money is given by 20 percent of the people. Go for them.

Retail organizations may spend 15 percent of their revenues on advertising, but that is high for a normal business. There is very little relation between the amount of advertising and the amount of business. A minimum amount will produce the same results as a maximum. It depends on how the advertising is placed. Use agencies if you can—they get their money from the media—but spend time making certain they understand your business. Don't assume it.

ALCOHOLICS

When I was working in the international scene, it sometimes seemed to me that half the people I knew were "functioning alcoholics," and several weren't functioning. I never met anyone booze improves, including me. Today it is not as acceptable in business to drink to excess. But if there are employees who have problems with alcohol, do not attempt to reform them. They must do that themselves. However, this can be helped along by providing a clear choice: "Get straight or get out. No *second* second chance." This will do a great deal of good for all involved.

ANALYSIS

Fiction is built around people who draw incorrect conclusions from an analysis of the data presented to them. In fiction it usually works out properly in the end, when the truth is revealed, and everyone lives happily ever after.

In business, an erroneous conclusion can lead to a disaster that precludes any happy endings. This is particularly true when the executives involved change things on the basis of current information only. People are laid off, locations are closed, and orders are canceled before any checking can be done. On the other hand, everything can be doubled just as quickly if the analysis is positive.

Running a business is like managing a flowing river. It moves all the time there is water in it. Measurements, such as depth, width, content, and speed, are combined with historical trends to let one know what the river is doing. Patterns of analysis have to be developed to let managers determine when a change is happening.

The successful executive combines a knowledge of the past with measurements of the present to develop a strategy of accomplishment for the future. All actions taken should be in harmony with this.

Analyze—don't guess or react to impulses.

APPRECIATION

The most desired of all responses is appreciation. Each of us wants others to recognize that we are valuable in some context and to let us know about it. Yet something in the human condition keeps us from taking the simple steps involved in showing or telling others that they make the world better for us. I remember a luncheon group of older mothers in the New York area named the "It Wouldn't Hurt You to Call Me Once in a While" Club. People band together in associations, clubs, lodges, and such in order to give and get awards as well as visibility. The need is real and permanent.

In any organization, it is the responsibility of the leader to recognize that this need exists and to conduct a regular review of the subject. The executive who says "They get paid for doing the job," or something along that line, is out of touch with reality.

Money does not serve as appreciation and is suspect even as a token. It is not personal enough and is no substitute for something that can be displayed or worn.

Put a few people together to think about the subject. Then you can determine what is considered proper in the culture of your organization.

ARTS

This refers to the various community organizations that support and put forth such activities as the symphony, ballet, art festival, and science center. All are nonprofit; all struggle along. Part of their financial problem is self-inflicted to the extent that they do not manage their internal affairs well; the rest comes from the community to the extent that it does not know how to deal with them. The arts have to be treated as businesses. The supporters have to be treated as customers.

For those who run worthwhile organizations, the more you know about efficient management, the tax laws, and appreciation, the better your organization will grow.

ASSISTANT TO

The "assistant to," or AT, is someone who is in training to become a professional and who possesses the basic skills or knowledge. No matter how well compensated, the AT is a helper, not an apprentice.

This is a valuable position for learning and making a contribution. An energetic AT will take a great many details off the boss's shoulders, will be forward-thinking, and will have a material effect on the entire organization.

ATs get into trouble when they forget the differences between their job and the jobs of the person they are assisting.

ATTITUDE

I really believe that bacteria and such don't make us sick until the way we look at things depresses the body's immune system and lets the "bugs" operate.

People deal with life according to the way they view it, and that view reflects their attitudes. These are negative or positive, depending on a vast combination of influences, both hereditary and environmental.

Attitudes can be modified, but rarely changed. It is best to select those people to work with us whose basic attitude comes close to what we are comfortable with.

Negative people can make positive people sick, and vice versa.

BIRTHDAYS

People never become so cynical that they stop thinking their birthday is a very special time. It is theirs; they don't care to share it with others having the same date. Organizations can make many points with their employees by buying them a lunch or encouraging some remembrance on that day.

BOARD OF DIRECTORS

Corporations, whether "for profit" or not, are required to have a board of directors. The idea is to have a group made up of well-qualified individuals who are not employees of the corporation to advise and direct the course of the operation. Board members do not deal with day-to-day affairs. The size of the board is up to the company.

Not-for-profit groups, such as hospitals or arts foundations, see their directors as providing fund-raising support as well as direction. Profit companies place individuals with ties to the business, such as suppliers, bankers, lawyers, or consultants, on their boards. This is usually not a good idea. A great deal of trouble can be averted by following the advice of directors who are not personally involved.

Directors can be personally liable for failure to take the job seriously. Many corporations purchase insurance to cover them. Boards usually meet at least once a quarter, and many meet monthly.

BONUS

It is not a good idea to give people bonuses. They are considered unstructured and emotional. Instead, use incentive compensation or profit sharing.

BORROWING

It has always been considered a good idea to do business using someone else's money. However, debt is not a friend. It is much better to have investments that do not need to be repaid. That is a good reason for going public.

If you must borrow, do it through a line of credit and keep it paid down. At least once a year, erase all debt. Resist the temptation to roll it over into long-term debt.

At any rate, do not get into a position where debt is more than 25 percent of assets.

BUDGETS, COMPANY

A budget is a communication system that was originally designed as an agreement between those who were going to spend the money and those who were going to provide it. By agreeing to the tasks involved and then to the funds required, the parties arrived at a functional plan that could be readily measured.

Unfortunately, budgeting became an art form when staff functions stepped in between the two forces. A great deal of energy is now placed on creating the budget—to show who has power—but very little on meeting it ("Any dummy can implement a well-thought-out budget").

The result has been that budgets, as a whole, are not taken seriously and no other usable system of control has emerged. That is why a great many organizations get into financial trouble without realizing it early enough.

BUDGETS, PERSONAL

To most individuals, budgets are a way of tracking overspending. Some people keep very neat records. Companies can overspend and work their way out of it. They can even declare a loss and move on to the next year. Individuals can't do that.

Budgeting is simply a plan for accomplishing personal goals. But, like dieting, it requires a dedication to the desired results that overcomes the temptation of the moment.

Budgets should be divided into two general areas: things you have to do (rent, food, utilities) and things you would like to do (clothes, eating out, travel, etc.).

CASH FLOW

The true measure of the value of an operation is the cash it generates that can be used for something other than running the business, paying taxes, and such. There are many definitions of cash flow, but it is generally felt to be cash from operations, less tax, less expenses that don't require cash (depreciation), plus accounts receivable, and adjusted to exclude long-term debt.

Discretionary cash flow from operations is minus capital items, short-term debt, and dividends.

How cash flow is figured is not as important as evaluating the changes in year-to-year status, keeping the same definition. That provides a good picture of how the operation is being managed. Cash is better than anything.

CASH MANAGEMENT

Looking into the future concerning expenses and figuring where the money to meet them is going to come from—that is cash management. If we are going to hire three more salespersons and it will take 6 months to make them capable of paying their own way, then we have to know where that 18 months of compensation and expenses will come from.

A company can get past practically every obstacle except running out of cash.

CEO

Chief executive officer. Where the buck stops. The person legally designated by the board of directors to act on its behalf. The CEO may delegate authority but always keeps the responsibility.

CHILD CARE

The typical company has many single parents who are faced with the problem of what to do with children during the day or after school. The company that helps these employees find and finance day care or after-school support (such as the "Y's" offer) will find itself paying a modest expense that produces more attentive and loyal employees. The majority of incoming and outgoing personal telephone calls are in reference to child care.

COMMITMENT

This is a popular word in organizations and refers to the amount of dedication management or individuals have to a specific goal or object. Commitment is judged by acts, not by words. The payroll is always met, but everything else may not be handled with the same intensity.

If someone questions your commitment to something, the proper response is, "What would I have to do to convince you I am serious about it?"

COMMITTEES

Contrary to belief, committees are a good management device. Provided with a proper charter and leadership, groups of people are the most effective way to get things done. Committee chairpersons require some training, and the groups who accomplish their tasks need appreciation.

Restock them once in a while.

COMMUNICATION

We talk more and do less about this subject than any other in business. That is because we really don't understand it. Each of us needs a sign on his or her desk saying: "Who else needs to know about this?"

Getting people to *want* to know is a large part of the communication battle. Information must be force-fed on a routine basis.

A meeting of all the staff at least once a month in a structured yet open setting is essential. This is in addition to the regular status meetings.

Try to determine who did not know what and why—so that corrective action can be taken. Most communication blocks occur because people didn't know an information source was available to them.

COMPETITION

People perform best when they feel they have some competition. Organizations that dominate their market or individuals who overpower their field have to create artificial competition.

This leads to internal groups going for the same goals and recognition. It generally results in more good news than bad.

When real competition exists, the competitors must be watched closely to ensure that their actions do not produce some unthought-of advantage. They can be held out in front to show that your zeal must be undiminished.

Never say anything bad about a competitor.

COMPENSATION

Money and other forms of payment received for work are called *compensation*. This also includes benefits, which account for 35 percent of total compensation. Total compensation in service companies should be about 50 percent of all expenses. In manufacturing companies it runs about 20 percent. A comparison of revenue per worker and compensation per worker is considered a good measure of how a company is doing. If the management resists taking action that will cause revenue per employee to fall below expenses per employee, the company will do well.

COMPUTERS

Right now, computers still have a mystique that places them outside the category of normal office equipment, but typewriters had a similar mystique at one time. Just as typewriters have not made letters clearer or shorter, computers have not made data less muddled. However, given a proper database and an unclouded eye, these machines can enable employees to do things they could never do before and to do them quickly. Computerization opens opportunities for better communication with clients and suppliers.

Put someone in charge of the system who speaks normal English and whose first goal is to do what you already do—but to do it better.

CONSULTANTS

Not every organization can contain within itself all the skills necessary to run a complex business. That is where consultants come in. However, they need to be hired for a purpose and to help accomplish a specific goal.

The most valuable consultants are those who specialize in one particular field and who learned their skills through actual practice in real life. They usually have a set format that needs to be followed in order to eliminate the problem and set the company up to handle similar problems on its own in the future.

Worry about consultants who advertise or solicit. "Internal" consultant organizations are useless.

CONTRACTS

Do not ever take a contract for granted; there is no such thing as a standard contract. Send each one to your attorney for comment and advice. The simpler contracts are not always the best. Keep in mind that contracts are communications documents which may be used by noninterested people to decide something. Contracts are supposed to bring businesses together on a subject, not provide a basis for argument.

In addition to the ones normally encountered in business, such as leases, other contracts are sometimes needed. Key employees may have contracts that protect both parties; suppliers are more reliable and cost-conscious when they have long-range agreements.

CONTRIBUTIONS

Giving help will make an organization feel good. Profit-making organizations that share with others in the community make it a better place in which to live. Contributions up to 10 percent of net profit can be deducted from tax returns. Employees should be invited to submit the names of their personal charities to make certain the contributions will be well-rounded. Their names can be included in the letters announcing the gifts.

Exclude neighborhood churches. Their congregations really do not want corporate help, and there are a great many of them.

To gain the proper recognition for the company, certain key and visible activities may be publicized. Set up a formal Contribution Committee to keep everyone participating.

CONVENTIONS

Conventions are formal programs held over several days that cover one subject or a group of subjects in great detail. They provide an opportunity for people with similar concerns to get together and be revitalized. The most important part of conventions goes on in the hallways and at the exhibits, where participants are brought up to date with the latest information. The value gained from advertising and presenting papers is very small.

CORRECTIVE ACTION

When problems occur, they must be fixed in two stages: First, deal with the current situation, somehow overcome it, and get things moving. Second, go back and look at the real cause, the "root cause," of the problem, and then figure out how to eliminate it forever.

Most problems have their origins in incomplete requirements or in incomplete understanding of the requirements somewhere up the line. It must be made very clear to everyone that we are trying to fight the problem, not the people. By following the trail back to its source, identifying the cause, and eliminating it, we serve our company well and avoid a great deal of frustration.

Companies need a formal system of corrective action that they can teach and repeat.

COUNSELING

I do not know of any time in life when a person cannot use counseling. Usually, counseling is thought of as negative or as something which indicates that you're sick. One case that comes to mind is the midlife crisis, which happens around 40 years of age. Each person who goes through it thinks he or she invented it. Counseling shows people that it is a normal part of life and can be handled.

CREATIVITY

Creativity is the ability to bring something into existence that was not there before. Each individual has his or her own streak of creativity, and some have it a great deal more than others. When such persons are found, they need to be pointed in a specific direction and then left alone. However, creativity is really part of normal activity.

To create something is one thing; to communicate what has been created to others so that they can utilize it is quite another. In this regard, creative people need to apply their most diligent activity in explaining the complicated in terms that can be readily understood and implemented. Do not let creative people feel that they can dream up a good idea and then dump it on somebody else to explain and implement. A creative idea is not in place until it can be accomplished in detail by untrained people.

CULTURE

Culture really is refinement. It is the predictable behavior in a group or an organization or people that is the result of the way they have been led to believe they work. Even more important is the way they have been exampled. People pretty much respond to what they see going on about them and copy that behavior, in some cases for good and in some cases for bad.

Each organization has its own culture, which is developed

very much by the values that are put forth by senior management. However, improved behavior and proper values, once explained, are usually accepted. Everyone has to learn to understand all of this in the same way and develop a common language.

CUSTOMERS

Customers, traditionally, are the ones who pay money to an organization for its products and services. However, there are other applications. In charities, customers are really two groups: (1) the ones who receive the benefits of the charity and (2) the ones who contribute. Both groups are to be dealt with.

Inside any organization, every person has a customer. It may not be the final one who gets the package. It can be the person at the next desk. It can be the person across town or across the nation. All of us need to identify our customers and make certain that we are satisfying them.

DECORATING

Every office, every organization, every factory, and every other entity needs to be decorated. Some thought should go into the selection of colors. This does not mean things need to be expensive, just that some consideration should be given to the harmony of the decorations.

The colors of the walls, and the artwork, speak very much for management's consideration of its employees. Also, many colors have been shown to have a negative effect on the work force.

DEVELOPMENT

There is no more urgent task than helping people to be more competent. Development is best done by management as a whole rather than by one group. Successful executives learn how to let people grow and prosper. Paying tuitions for employees to study whatever they want to study is not very expensive and is a very fine motivator. The way to measure development is to see whether people are able to perform a job that gave them a great deal of difficulty a year ago in half the time.

DEVELOPMENT, PRODUCT

Product development has to be done on a planned basis after a need is identified by marketing or customer input or analysis. Project management has to be set up to create a product that will fulfill the requirements.

Creative people need to be scheduled and left alone, but without controls, the costs will soon be out of line.

Product development has to be forced. It must be thought out, planned, and made to happen. There is no company that can continue having the same product year after year without change. Ford made the Model T for 18 years and would not change it despite continuing evidence that the public would have liked a little variety. When it finally did change to the Model A, it was never able to regain its market share. It was just too late.

Development is not complete until the product can pass all the tests that prove it will perform to all the prescribed requirements.

DISCIPLINE

It is not necessary to have bullwhips and hobnail boots to have discipline. Discipline is a matter of attitude; it relates to pride in performance generated by management's attitude. It involves such things as arriving at work on time, getting the reports produced completely, and meeting other obligations routinely. All individuals are subject to the same discipline in the well-run organization.

DISCRIMINATION

The business of not treating someone differently because of age, sex, color, or whatever, is very difficult. It is difficult because just the simple thought causes some discrimination, whether intended or not. The best way to guard against this is to have continual reviews on a planned basis by objective people.

Discrimination is not the problem that it used to be because everyone is very much aware of it. Awareness is the way to keep it from happening. People who continually use either racial or sexist comments in their conversation should be firmly told, "We do not do that around here."

DRESS CODE

Discretion requires that people dress in accordance with the culture they live in. Many companies have established dress codes but find them difficult to enforce. A solution is to assemble a group of individuals representing the different age groups and ask them for their suggestions. They will usually come up with something that is relatively mild and bland, and the company will probably decide not to have a formal code. Once the awareness is evident, things will correct themselves, particularly if the management of the company dresses properly in order to set an example.

If it can be worked out, a uniform or company clothing of some sort among the lower levels of an organization will be well accepted.

DRUG ABUSE

Abuse of other forms of drugs besides alcohol is becoming more prevalent nowadays. Many of the users are subtle in their usage, and such things as cocaine and marijuana are not all that easy to detect. Information seminars should be arranged. Managers and supervisory personnel will have to develop an awareness of whether their employees are having problems with drugs. Companies need drug abuse prevention programs. They also need to know how to get drug abusers to treatment. I think it has to be recognized that anybody can develop a drug problem; in many cases it is the people we are least likely to expect.

EDUCATION

This is an incredibly broad subject. It is something that every company and organization wants to encourage employees to get more of. Strangely enough, many companies make it difficult for this to happen. In order to provide tuition reimbursement, for instance, they require proof that each course taken will relate directly to the individual's job. I believe that employees have a better chance to develop the education habit if companies help pay for any course, including basket weaving, that people want to take.

The educational needs of each employee should be noted as part of his or her professional review. Some courses relating to the particular business of an organization can be taught internally.

People should be encouraged to read widely and to study what they wish—just to study.

EGO

The single most repetitive cause of failure in executive ranks, or failure of a corporation, is management ego. Some people can very quickly begin to think that they are vitally important and irreplaceable. However, many corporations are run and many special businesses happen all over the world without these particular people. So, for that reason alone, they just may not be irreplaceable. Ego is something that we feel other people have; we do not believe we have it, and we do not recognize it when it is there. Ego is with the individual, with the head of the company, and with the other people.

This is what boards of directors are for. It is up to the board to recognize when the senior executives of the company lose touch with reality and are mainly involved in their own aggrandizement. At that moment, the board must caution them, warn them, and—if all else fails—get rid of them if the company is to survive. Ego is an incredibly serious problem.

Ego and self-confidence are at opposite ends of the scale.

ENTREPRENEUR

"Someone who starts a business" is a very shallow definition because an entrepreneur is really an idea person who implements. People who are willing to take risks with their own personal resources and time in order to accomplish ideas or objectives that they hold very dear are true entrepreneurs. They are recognizable because of the tendency to forge ahead whether or not appropriate money and backing are available.

Pseudo entrepreneurs spend all their time trying to raise money, making certain that very little of it is their own.

The conventional concept of entrepreneurs is that there is very little control involved and that risks are taken on hunches. Actually, the opposite is true, as things are very well thought out.

The time may come when an entrepreneur loses interest in the operation. After it becomes routine, he or she may want to pursue new ideas. When that begins to happen, the entrepreneur is wise to turn the management over to someone else and get out of the way.

The opposite occurs when the founder will not let anyone else really run anything; the company begins to strangle because its growth is limited.

EXECUTIVES

Executives are the people who create the decisions and the situations that are to be carried out by managers. The successful executive is able to comprehend detail and deal with it to the extent necessary to understand the situation and not be overwhelmed by it. Executives make decisions which are based on fact, experience, and intuition. The difference between a successful and an unsuccessful executive lies in the ability to communicate. Very few executives can make a good speech.

EXPENSES

Expenses are one of the characteristics of producing materials and services that are sold to provide revenue. As a group, expenses are looked at in a negative way; that is, expenses are automatically bad. Usually this translates to the "out of profit" charges for traveling, eating, or dealing with daily cash needs. These can be predicted and controlled. I can make out an expense report 6 months in advance and get it all right.

FADS

Management, particularly American management, is obsessed with fads. Managers learn to deal with the "silver bullet" that will solve any problem with little effort. Unfortunately, most fads are directed at the symptom rather than the cause. The cause, in most cases, is the attitude or understanding of the managers, and their normal inclination, of course, is to look somewhere else for the solution.

A fad can be recognized by the way it bursts suddenly upon the scene from out of nowhere. It arrives full-blown, implemented by those who advocate it and criticized by those who don't. There seems to be no foundation for its having grown in a methodical manner. But somewhere beneath every fad is a truth that needs to be recognized. Search for that, and the concept involved will become something, when applied, which will improve the management style of the organization.

"Quality circles" come to mind along this line. The idea that the lower-level people of the organization can solve the management-caused problems of the quality organization is ridiculous. But the idea of getting people together to talk about problems and identify possible improvements in the operation is solid.

FAILURE

Like success, failure does not always lead to improvement. Yet from the ashes of failed projects many great ventures have arisen. Failure is in the mind only, since we do not know enough about the future. We do not know what tomorrow will bring so we often give up on something too soon.

Improvements in management capability come from learning through failing. Finding out what does not work is as important as finding out what does.

FAMILY COUNCIL

As chairman of PCA, I conduct monthly meetings where all employees gather together in one room to go over the activities of the company. As companies grow larger, this is not always practical, but smaller units can do the same thing. Information can be passed on from other levels in the form of videotapes.

In these open sessions, each department and division gives a report on its status. The controller reviews finances; Human Resources talks about benefits or other programs; and individual departments give special reports on what they have been doing. Awards, such as 5-year pins, are passed out during these meetings.

Questions asked from the floor or written prior to the meetings are discussed openly by the senior executives, and everything is answered to everybody's satisfaction. The result of the Family Council, which takes an hour and a half a month, is that participants feel they have the opportunity to communicate and understand. Also, the meetings are very upbeat and motivational sessions.

FIELD SERVICE

This used to be a noble profession, the business of keeping operational the equipment customers had purchased from a company. Now we know that, if run that way, field service is a repair station, is very expensive, and does not make real money or reputation for the company.

Field service should help customers get the best use out of their equipment and occasionally provide advice about new equipment that can make things even better for them. Never form a company with field service as a start-up operation. It will never end.

FINANCIAL CONTROL

More companies go down the chute because of improper control of the money they had than because of lack of money. It does not require a great many controls in order to know the status.

First of all, we need revenues so that we know how much is coming in; accounts receivable so that we know how much we are owed; accounts payable so that we know how much we have going out to our suppliers, employees, and other people; and expenses. Probably a dozen categories of expenses need to be noted. There are fixed expenses such as compensation, rent, leases, and equipment. There are variable expenses such as travel, conferences, and education.

A simple list showing what is available and what is being expended should be made up on a weekly basis (some companies do it only monthly) to see where you are. I often think that how close the leader is to these numbers is a sign of the growth and prosperity of the company.

In the early days of a company the leader knows where every penny is at any given moment. As prosperity sets in and things become more regimented, it is possible that the leader will deal with the top numbers only. This is something that is probably necessary, but it sure takes the emphasis off financial control.

The status of finances should be made known to much lower levels within the company than it usually is. One of the reasons people spend money without thinking about it is that they do not think it relates to them.

FIRING

Every now and then, someone does not fit into the organization and has to be let go. Unless there is some cause involved, such as fraud or another method of betraying a trust, firing should be considered a very serious matter. The act of terminating somebody from a company involves more than severing the relationship between an individual and a company. It also makes other people nervous.

The main thing that should come out of a firing is an understanding of where the selection process went wrong (what let that person be hired in the first place) or of where the training and discipline activities of the company were inadequate. Firing should be done as graciously as possible and with as little pain to employees as possible. They should be sent out into the world without condemnation and without any lack of references. Some managers are super impatient or do not have the means to do proper evaluation. If more than 1 percent of a company's population is fired in a year, there is a very severe problem.

FLOAT

While checks and other items are being processed through banks, credit card companies, and other financial institutions, that money is not available to its owner. However, the financial institution is busily loaning out that very money or gaining interest on the funds those checks represent. That is *float*.

It is estimated that some traveler's check companies have $6 billion at any given moment because until travelers cash their checks, the company receives interest on them.

In managing the financial affairs of a company, it is good to recognize that float exists. It is possible to arrange with a bank to have funds protected so that they can always be actively working for the company. This means that what is in the bank account and the checking account can be invested at night and over the weekend, for instance, instead of sitting for 10 or more days.

FOUNDERS

Those who start up a company are known as the *founders*. However, not everyone who starts up a company is a founder. Founders are the ones who use personal financial resources and who have bet their lives. They are people who come to work at the beginning for no money, hock their houses, and put integrity into the operation.

FREIGHT

Freight is the commodity of transportation. The most interesting thing about it is that the one receiving the material pays the freight bill. Therefore, we want to be very careful about how we designate something to be sent to us. The most rapid way is not always the most practical or expensive.

These days, when everybody wants to have a minimal amount of inventory, pickups and deliveries are scheduled on an hourly basis. Freight firms are given schedules in advance, and they are assigned specific times of the day when they can unload pickups from suppliers at the warehouses or even at seminars.

Just-in-time strategies lower inventory holding costs, but they also run up the cost of freight. Overnight and other rapid express shipments are being used routinely and have lost much of their value. People just assume they have a few days' extension on the schedule.

GIFTS

No executive should receive gifts from anybody in the company or from its suppliers. Gifts imply a *pro quid pro.*

However, when dealing with companies in the Far East, we must recognize that it is a part of the custom in most Far Eastern countries to give gifts to friends and to business acquaintances. These gifts really don't mean that much in themselves, because they are hardly ever unwrapped and may even be passed on to the next giftee.

When you are traveling in the Far East or greeting oriental guests, it is a nice thought to have small presents available. Items with your company's monogram on them will be appreciated mementos.

Gifts should be given in relation to an individual's relative level of importance in the company. The careers of lower-level employees can be destroyed if they receive more valuable or larger gifts than their seniors.

GRAPEVINE

Studies always show that the biggest source of information inside any company is the grapevine. The grapevine can be encouraged and used, if necessary, by putting out information about the company through a newspaper, Family Council, or other means of internal communication. Gossip is mischievous at best. It often happens because the senior managers of the company are gossips themselves or because they encourage it, listen to it, or do not make a big deal about discouraging it.

I find that mentioning during the initial orientation that we don't gossip about each other, or our clients, has a good effect. Usually companies do not talk about that sort of thing; it's under the surface. But bringing it up on top, and then saying that it is bad for us and bad for the company and that employees really can ask about anything and get an answer, will tend to cut it down. However, do not forget that gossiping is probably the number-one interest of most human beings.

GRAPHICS

The main thing to know about graphics is that they are a lot more complicated and take a lot more time than is generally thought. One of the main reasons that reports, covers, or brochures are late is because not enough time is given for the graphics to be done properly. Good and on-time graphics require up-front agreement between the artist and the requester on what has to be done. It should all be put in writing.

GROWTH, COMPANY

The company that does not grow each year in revenue and profit is headed for trouble. The reason for this is that expenses are going to rise a little bit every year because producers cannot increase prices as the prices of the services they use are increased. Therefore, productivity must improve every year in order to meet the demands of the business.

Unfortunately, some companies try to force this growth by artificial means, such as acquisitions. Acquisitions provide temporary relief because the earnings and the revenue of another company are absorbed. However, debt and goodwill require expenses that may drag it all down. A company should grow because it has products and services customers want, not because somebody has an ego trip.

Just taking care, or planning well, does not seem to cause growth. There has to be a sound product, a striving organization, and leadership with integrity. A company grows at its own rate, which only changes when the company becomes too cumbersome to manage.

GROWTH, PERSONAL

All individuals have to be concerned with expanding their knowledge and information bases in learning how to deal with the world. From going to Toastmasters to learn how to speak, to setting the "Fog Index" when they write, to learning how to dress properly to present themselves, all individuals have to take this very seriously. No one else is going to do much about it.

The biggest single problem people have in the area of personal growth is learning how to solicit and accept and examine advice as it comes to them. If individuals are lucky enough to find wise persons who will take interest in them, then they have mentors. Mentors are very valuable because they have been through all of it before and can pass some of their experience along. This does not mean that individuals should do everything their mentors say, but they should certainly take advantage of their mentors' experience.

Personal goals are as important as company goals. Nothing will happen unless individuals have something they want to accomplish and go for it.

HIRING

I believe that the leader should have at least a 2-minute interview with everybody the operation is seriously considering hiring, if only to see that the applicant's personality will fit. People should be selected very carefully because they are going to be around for a long time. They should be interviewed by at least three levels of supervision and a peer or two. They should come back for a second interview and be asked all the specific questions possible under the equal employment laws. As to the number of people to hire, we should never hire people when doing so would reduce the revenue per employee, and we should hire people only when there are actual jobs to do, not when we are betting on the future.

HUMAN RESOURCES

Human resources departments attempt to handle the relations between a company and its employees on the basis of the fact that the employees really are a valuable resource of the company, not just something said to be a valuable resource. The structure necessary to manage this function is personnel, industrial relations, wellness centers, child care, medical insurance, and so on.

One problem is that professionals in this field don't seem very sensitive to the people. They are much more sensitive to the needs of administration. This is because they have not learned to administer and still be empathetic at the same time. Human resources departments often state that the majority of complaints they hear are about the way their companies treat people.

Human resources needs to lead the way in relations by helping to cause clear understandings about company policies and practices. Then the employees can have some input.

INTERNAL REVENUE SERVICE

The big difference between for-profit and not-for-profit organizations is that for-profit organizations have to take the revenue code into consideration on almost every business decision they make. This is also the reason business managers do not do as well when they get into nonprofit organizations.

Internal Revenue does not make laws, it just enforces the ones that are made by our elected representatives, who go to Washington to terrorize us in this manner. My feeling about taxes is pay them and move on.

INTERNATIONAL

This really should be "World." We have to learn to think of everything in terms of the world environment and not just the local jurisdiction. People who run charitable organizations in the middle of Illinois, for instance, can learn from people who are doing similar things in France or Asia or other far-off places.

Very few companies are not affected by the international actions in their fields. If they do not learn how to be "movers," they will be "shaken."

When setting up a location in another country, hire locals, train them in your shop for 6 months, and then support them properly as they set up the office. Expatriates do not feel natural or comfortable; most of them never learn how to operate in their adopted country.

INTERVIEW

The big problem with interviews is that they are usually one-shot deals. To interview people who are going to be important in life, it is necessary to learn how they will relate to several areas. It is almost like a courtship. There are very few people left whose first impression always turns out to be the correct one. I'm not sure that that ever worked in the first place.

It takes a while to get to know other people, and I think a great deal of pain in the executive world could be prevented with proper interviewing. Psychological testing has very little value; the devious learn how to manipulate it.

INVENTORY

Inventory is whatever an operation needs in order to produce. In manufacturing companies it is usually seen stacked in a warehouse or get-ready place or in between job operations, and it has always been considered an essential part of doing business. The main reason it is there is because the quality is not dependable, which means backup is needed. Now we are beginning to realize that it is not necessary to have all that inventory stacked up waiting in order to keep the operation from misfiring.

Service companies do not think of themselves as having inventory and paying interest on the holding costs. Actually, they have to look at programming efforts, product development, program development, and training as an inventory of sorts. All are things that are built up prior to doing actual work.

The entire concept of inventory has been changing back to what it originally was in Henry Ford's day, when there were daily deliveries to the plants. Also at that time, machines were very close together in machine shops, so there was no in-process inventory being moved around by forklift trucks and such. Now, we are returning to that system, and the business of managing inventory has changed to the business of eliminating inventory.

JAPAN

Between the end of World War II and the present time, this fascinating nation has probably done the biggest turnaround in the history of the world. Japan has gone from near-complete desolation to being a very large economic influence in the world. The Japanese owe their success to being very smart and working hard. Yet, there seems to be a paradox. They are much more successful out in the rest of the world than they are inside Japan. The majority of companies inside Japan are not very well managed and are not all that successful. Their bankruptcy rate is comparable to that of companies in the rest of the world.

The large export companies have learned to mass-produce excellent products by adhering to the standard of zero defects. They make this happen through management integrity and through a system that lets total up-front agreement be a normal practice.

Japan faces many problems and should become less of an economic force over the next two or three decades. The nation has an aging work force, an unprofitable consumer market, and almost no immigration; and it has not been very successful in exporting management techniques throughout Asia. However, the Japanese are an industrious people and will be heard from.

JOB DESCRIPTIONS

This quaint habit from the past is something that should be, and happily is being, cheerfully revived. The thought that managers actually have to describe what they want workers to do somehow got lost over the last 20 years. Today, managers and workers are sitting together, writing job descriptions, and coming to an agreement, an understanding, on them. This produces conformance to the requirements, which means that all the people involved understand what they are supposed to do. Everybody does it, and all the work comes out the way it should. Job descriptions should not be incredibly formal; they should just be complete.

JOB SHARING

It is possible to take many jobs and divide them into halves. For instance, one person can answer the switchboard all morning, and another person can answer the switchboard all afternoon; that can be each one's complete job. This lets people with children or other responsibilities have employment, earn a good salary, and receive benefits without neglecting those duties that are important to them. Many companies immediately say that they can't do this sort of thing, but they really can.

KANBAN

"Kanban" is a Japanese word for zero inventory. What this means is that work is planned so that suppliers produce and deliver a certain amount of inventory every day at a certain time, directly to the production lines. As a result, manufacturers do not have to store inventory, do not have to pay the interest on it, and, in this way, can be much more efficient. They also have to be willing to recognize that once in a while they may have to stop the line or hold it up and that if this happens, they should not make a big deal about it. Otherwise, somebody might start storing up inventory.

The bad side is that the suppliers essentially wind up paying for some inventory because they sometimes have to get backups in order to deliver at the proper times. Also, the freight firms have higher expenses since they are traveling the same distances with smaller loads.

LAYOFFS

When an organization has financial difficulties, one of the actions usually taken is to lay off employees. One of the problems with this is that it creates an internal morale and security problem that may far override the financial difficulties. It is much better, if possible, to deal with the situation in two steps.

First, take the people who should have been fired because they are nonperformers and get rid of them. This should be done on all levels: executives, managers, supervisors, employees, professionals, everybody. Pick out the people who are really not carrying their loads and lay them off as gently as possible. This will reduce compensation, and it will also let people know the situation is serious. They know who the nonperformers are.

Second, take the remaining employees and put them on a reduced week, such as a 4-day week. Everybody. Have the senior executives take a more dramatic pay cut, perhaps a third of their salaries. Bring all the employees together regularly and let them know what is happening. Show them what they need to do. Give them pep talks, but always tell them the truth. The turnaround will come much more dramatically and with greater firmness than otherwise.

Massive layoffs of, say, 20 percent of the work force can set a company back 20 years. Think about that when hiring people.

LEASES

Never sign a lease until your lawyer has read it. Try not to include articles in the lease that automatically increase the rent or the fee or whatever is involved unless they give some benefit in return. Do not sign a lease brought by the experts hired to prepare it without sending it to your attorney. Remember that a lease really is a capital item, even though it is an agreement to pay over a period of time. A 5-year lease commitment to pay somebody $20,000 a year for building rent is a $100,000 commitment. It is the same thing as a $100,000 debt from the bank, which we know must be repaid.

LECTURE

The word "lecture" brings to mind a dull, droning session in a college classroom, where "the instructor's notes are passed to the student's notes without going through the head of either." What we want "lecture" to project is the thought of an exchange of information between interested parties. For this reason, lecturing must be taken very seriously and looked at as a presentation. Most of the traditional advice on lecturing is not very good. It has more to do with the material than with relating to the audience. The most important part of any lecture is the audience, not the lecturer or the material. Most poor lecturing is done because it is thought that the material can stand on its own.

LENDING

My personal recommendation is never lend money to anybody, particularly relatives. If the desire to help them out is overwhelming, then just give it to them.

LETTERS

Most business letters are terrible. They contain words that people do not use in conversation and are structured, stilted, and unfriendly. Letters should not be "good-old-boy" jovial types, but they also don't need to sound like they were dictated by an Oxford don to his solicitor. Courses for letter writers given by local college professors are very helpful. It is also a good idea to study the "Fog Index."

LOUNGE, EMPLOYEE

Organizations should have a place or places set aside where employees can go to sit down and relax for a few minutes. The lounge should have smoking and nonsmoking areas. Profitable companies provide a refrigerator and keep it stocked with juice.

The lounge is a good place for a bulletin board that carries personal announcements by the employees. Executives should share the same lounge. They will go there only often enough to keep it from becoming a place where people "hang out." Executives have their own offices, which they can turn into lounging areas if they wish. Do not give them a separate lounge. It is hard enough to get them to see the other people.

MAGAZINES

Every industry, profession, region, city, and organization has its own magazine. These magazines limit discourses primarily to what is happening or significant in their particular areas of interest. People who are going to run something need a much broader understanding of the world than they can get from specialized magazines. While reading them, they should also reach out to daily national newspapers such as *The Wall Street Journal* and *The New York Times*; to management magazines such as *Forbes, Fortune,* and *Business Week*; and to a world news magazine such as *Time* or *The Economist.* In this worldwide business community we live in, it is just not possible to be limited in information and still be able to function.

Since no one really knows which information is important, the leader has to take a look at everything. I got one of my best ideas from the back of a breakfast cereal carton.

MANAGEMENT STYLE

This is another popular phrase that has come to mean a recognizable way of managing that can be attributed to a specific organization or individual. Books have been written with very thoughtful contents about the varying styles of managers and the varying results that they get.

To get things done, it is necessary to have a system. When something or someone comes in one door and goes out another, the process is handled in a prescribed way. But I have seen organizations with documented systems and no pattern of success. The Navy, for instance, operates to a well-described and specific system. Yet one ship is effective and happy, while another ship is ineffective and unhappy.

The key to management style is the relations of the senior executives to the people they are supervising. When they are able to create in those people the need to accomplish plus the feeling of appreciation and to provide them with the proper tools and instructions, the operation will be a success. The management style that pays off is one that is people-oriented and, at the same time, knows how to use technical applications. People really are the most important of all components.

A manager's style is the reflection of what he or she believes.

MANAGER

A manager is one who causes to be implemented what an executive has directed. Managers take people, budgets, and time and work all of them with and against each other in order to accomplish specific jobs. Many people with executive titles are managers. My feeling is that people are born either executives or managers and that it is possible to tell which they are by the time they are 3 years old. This does not mean they will ever get that title on the door at the proper age.

Hardly anyone else believes this.

MANUAL, OPERATING

If an organization is to have unity and do things in a routine way, it needs a manual of procedures, policies, and basic information for reference.

The items contained in the manual are not the kinds of things used on a day-to-day basis; rather, they serve to stop arguments and settle discussions. When employees come to work for the first time, they should be given operating manuals of their own. These should be serialized and kept up to date.

The real concern comes with what to put in the manual. Obviously, senior management has to make the policies. These should be in the front of the manual, and each policy should be no more than a sentence or two. We have policies on finance, quality, vacation, organization, hiring, and so on.

Procedures should be prepared by the people who are doing the jobs. Then they should be reviewed and approved by the Procedures Committee and put in the book. That way they have credibility. If we just dump something written by a manager in there, nobody will believe it and nobody will pay any attention to it.

"Conformance to requirements" starts with procedures.

MARGIN

Roughly, margin is the difference between the cost of output plus cost of sales and the actual price the customer pays. It is a little more than pretax profit. It is a mistake to take the cost of producing something and then add on a standard margin to determine the price. The price should be whatever is the right price for the item.

The cost of preparing or producing something has nothing to do with the price unless the cost comes out to be higher than the price acceptable to the customers. This is a different problem.

MARKETING

Positioning the product or service in the proper place in the market or business and presenting it in such a way that people become customers are what marketing is all about. Marketing people do not like to admit that they have anything to do with sales, but obviously the whole purpose of marketing is to create a situation in which a sale can be made.

In another sense, marketing is what we all do with our personal careers. Success or failure in the business world depends to a great degree on third-person credibility. The same is true in charitable organizations. For instance, the symphony that is thought of as a money-grubbing, disgruntled group of musicians gets very little support. The symphony that is thought of as yearning to pour music into the heart of every citizen receives all the funds and help it can handle. The difference between the two is marketing.

Companies such as Nieman-Marcus and Lazarus have developed a reputation for taking back whatever you bring them even if they didn't sell it to you. The reality is that this hardly ever happens, but the image of it is priceless. Such images are not generated by accident.

In careers, if one is thought of as a person of integrity, resourceful, energetic, and with an intense view of work, one will get far in the business world. If one is thought of as cantankerous, lazy, and difficult, obviously the reverse will be true. The difference in these two images lies very much in the hands of the individual. So all of us, as well as our businesses, need to think out how we wish to be presented to the world.

MBA

Master of Business Administration. This term has taken on a completely new meaning, separate from the academic degree itself. MBA has come to mean somebody with special skills learned during a graduate program. Certainly, the effort that is put forth to earn an MBA is worth recognizing. It is my belief that people should take an undergraduate degree in liberal arts, work 2 or 3 years, and then take an MBA. Then they will be prepared to survive and prosper in the business world.

Executive MBA programs are offered by many MBA schools today. These are for folks who are at a more senior level in their companies, who perhaps have reached the ripe old age of 35, 45, or such, and who would like to get their MBA. They go to school on alternate Fridays and Saturdays and have a couple of weeks a year in residence. This provides them with an MBA degree in 2 years, which is probably more meaningful than the ordinary MBA because of the experience of the classmates.

MEASUREMENT

No executive can make a proper decision without understanding the status of the organization, where it is going, and where it has been. This status comes from measurement—measurement of finances, products, services, customers, and other sources of activity.

Every company has different measurements. These can be concocted rather quickly by thinking of the process model, which says (1) that all work is a process and (2) that each person or activity receives inputs which are measurable, does some work which is measurable, and produces a result which is measurable. We can look at these and know where the job is going.

Senior managers need graphs, where they can see whether a line is going up or going down. The key thing about measurement is that it should be done in an objective and positive manner.

Measurements have to have integrity. If they change every now and then, people just do not believe them. The annual report is a gathering of measurements. Sometimes there are so many measurements that it is very hard to make judgments about what is going on. That is not the kind of information that executives need on a day-to-day basis.

MEDIA

This is a modern word, loosely defined as all the public information systems, such as television, radio, newspapers, and magazines. The public, customers, and competitors all receive information about organizations from the media. By the same token, organizations are the ones that supply a great deal of the information to the media, either directly or indirectly.

It is necessary to be very careful about what goes out and what is put out and also to be very practical about it. Organizations cannot hide from the media, and when they solicit the media, they get the opportunity to make big mistakes. Media people, for the most part, are very professional, are interested only in telling interesting stories, and are not out to "get any-body." However, organizations must deal with the media on a planned basis. Leave nothing to chance.

If a suitable consulting firm is not available or affordable, at least appoint a spokesperson. Think out what needs to be said on a subject and write it down. Then send that short comment to the media.

If a personal appearance is required, get a little coaching on how to do that sort of thing.

The images of companies, as well as those of individuals, are created in great part by what is written and said about them. We all know that, but we sometimes forget that poor information originates with ourselves.

MEETINGS

One of the myths of management is that meetings are a gigan-tic waste of time. This is because, for the most part, they are disoriented and disjointed and never stick to the subject. Also, people with poor meeting manners or Machiavellian tenden-cies dominate the meetings. Very little is accomplished. Most people prefer to make decisions on their own or perhaps to have a hallway session with somebody else and come to some kind of conclusion.

However, the well-run organization has a specific set of meetings for the purpose of communication and decision. These will add a great deal to the possibility of success if a few simple rules are followed: First, the meeting must have an agenda. Everybody has the opportunity and the responsibility to add things to the agenda. If a topic is not on the agenda, do not talk about it. This teaches people to get their thoughts in ahead of time. Second, the meeting must have a start time and a finish time. These have to be adhered to religiously. The chairperson of the meeting is in charge of the meeting; if sen-ior people are attending, they have to recognize this and defer to the chairperson. Presentations to the meeting should be pre-pared and rehearsed in advance, be concise and to the point, and give all the participants the opportunity to have their questions answered.

For a typical organization, I would suggest the following program: Weekly staff meetings should be held for each function, in which status is reviewed, action items are covered, and problems are assigned for corrective action. For the organization as a whole, there should be monthly Executive Committee meetings, attended by senior people representing every area. Plan to cover everything in an hour and a half. The Finance Committee should meet once a month; the board of directors, quarterly. The Procedures Committee should meet on a planned basis. The Integrity Board should meet once a month and take action. When a problem arises that requires action, a special team may be put together. This team should have regular status meetings every day at 8 A.M. for 45 minutes. The team members go over what is going on, what is supposed to happen, and what happened yesterday until they get the problem solved, congratulate each other, and do not meet anymore.

Meetings are a valuable part of an organization's management style. Only poorly managed meetings are not useful.

MINORITIES

Legally, minorities are women, people with Spanish surnames, and blacks. However, there are many more minorities in the world: short people, tall people, people with glasses, people who stutter, people who are left-handed, people with strange accents, people who are fat, people who are incredibly skinny, people who are fantastic golfers or athletes, people who jog, people who are great chefs or writers. In fact, everybody is a minority in some way. Not all these minorities suffer because of preconceived notions that other people have about them. But we have all been through it in some way, so we should have empathy for those whom bigots persecute. There is no excuse for making some people feel that they are different.

In business and charitable organizations, it is necessary to reach out to these people. They should be moved into positions that they may not have previously been able to reach because of unfair practices or other reasons.

MIS

Management information systems is a broad term that refers to what goes into the computer and comes out of the computer. Back in the days when we had pencils and papers and typewriters and such, it was not necessary to have MIS because everybody understood how to make the system work. Now, when everything comes off a data base, we have to be certain that the overall system is compatible with itself and other systems. It is very difficult to find people who understand electronics, understand management, and still can get along with everybody.

MIS should be a separate function reporting, depending on the size of the organization, to the controller or director of administration. If MIS reports to someone at the very top of the organization, they develop an entire world of their own; the series of connecting links around the system becomes very expensive, and the results are not much better than they were without MIS. I have seen it happen several times.

I do not see how any organization is going to be able to operate at all in the next 10 years without a competent MIS function. Smaller operations can buy a setup and hire someone temporarily to get it running.

MONEY

The funny thing about organizations and money is that they all know exactly how much they took in and spent. It is all written down, but you never see any actual money. I worked for a corporation with sales of $20 billion, and the only time I ever saw any honest-to-goodness cash was when I took it out of my pocket to buy a newspaper or tip a hotel attendant. What this means is that money is a concept, not a reality. It is a way of keeping score. Too important to be left sitting around, it is always being invested over the weekend or overnight. So when we talk about money, we should really be concerned about the use of money and its importance as a source of jobs and power.

MOTEL

Motels have gotten a bad name over the years because they are thought to be rather casual about their admittance policies, not necessarily very efficient, and not always very comfortable, quiet, or private. There is some truth in this, but they also fulfill a legitimate business need, since travel is essential to many businesses.

MOTIVATION

Executives would like to have a way of getting their people charged up to do good work with no effort on their part. Salespeople have meetings and tools and contests forever for this purpose.

Motivation, however, is almost always a short-term thing in itself, and it needs to be recognized as such. For instance, as professional golfers get older, their common complaint is that they have a hard time keeping charged up for 4 days in a row while they play a tournament. They miss out by just a few shots each time. Motivation programs are almost always a disappointment because they do not have real substance.

Genuine motivation comes from the way people feel they are treated and the witness that management presents. "Pride in work" is the result of "pride in employee."

People respond to what is around them. Crisis often brings out the best in people, while success may bring out the worst.

MYTHS

There are a lot of myths in management. When myths are repeated often enough, people begin to think that they are real. For instance, many believe the myth that Wall Street people and economists know more about the market (what is going to go up and down and what will make money) than other people know. Yet reality shows that they do not. The test, of course, is whether they know what the market is going to do tomorrow. If they do, then they really understand.

People who run small businesses and people who don't have a great deal of experience tend to think that everyone else knows a lot more than they do, that other people have secret sources of information, and so on. This really is just not true. An individual executive's judgment is as good as anyone else's. It is simply a matter of getting enough information to know what has gone wrong in the past. For instance, it is not necessary to be a genius to know that if one borrows money at 20 percent and then works to make a 10 percent return, the effort is going to sink slowly into the sea. Management gets into more trouble by listening to the superstitions of business than in any other way.

In volunteer organizations, this is particularly true. People tend to have fixed ideas, such as "The people of this community will not support a symphony because they do not like good music." How does anybody know that? It only takes a certain portion of any community to provide the funding and attendance needed to accomplish something. It is a matter of finding the right people and reaching them. So rather than assuming that something cannot be done, gather some data or take a survey. Years ago, when I developed an award program for ITT which was based on lapel pins and rings, everyone told me the Europeans would not go for that sort of thing. As a matter of fact, they were the biggest advocates of the program. People sometimes forget that armies are built around medals of recognition.

OFFICE SPACE

Many organizations provide cramped office conditions for their employees because they think they are saving money and improving efficiency by having everybody closer together. As a matter of fact, such closeness makes people uncomfortable. Space in offices should be about the same as in homes, which means that people should have enough room to do their thing.

Out in the open areas, the desks should be at least 3 feet apart. Individual offices should be at least 120 square feet, with a desk and a couple of chairs. Larger offices can have a table and a sofa. There should be only two sizes of offices: larger offices for senior executives who have a lot people reporting to them (so that they can have meetings in their offices of, say, six people) and smaller offices for workers who talk with two or three people at a time.

Individuals should be allowed to pick their office furniture, within a budget, as much as possible, recognizing that when somebody leaves somebody else is going to inherit that furniture.

Offices should be decorated in pleasant, soft colors—tending toward the browns and roses—so that people are comfortable. Offices should have padded carpets and be treated as nice places to be, not just as money factories.

Department stores figure sales per square foot of office space. That's not a bad thing to do for a business office. How much revenue are we getting per square foot? If we are going to add more space, are we going to get revenue out of it? This does not contradict what I said before, because there have to be certain basic rules of space per person. In most productive offices I have seen, there is plenty of room to walk around and plenty of room for people to be alone if they wish to be.

OFFICE SUPPLIES

Someone should be put in charge of office supplies. There should be a central storage area where people can get what they need and take it back to their desks. Leaders should recognize the need to be thrifty in the use of supplies. It is not all that valuable but it is highly visible and sets a good example.

ORGANIZATION

Some organizations pride themselves on not having an organization chart. All this does is produce confusion. The purpose of an organization chart is merely to establish lines of communication. There should be several basic rules. One is that people should report to one boss although they may have others whom they contact to clear certain information. All bosses should have at least five or six people reporting to them. One over one is an absolute no-no, and one over two creates rivalries.

I remember a college campus where they put in six buildings and did not put in the paths connecting any of them. They planted all the grass and let the students and faculty go from building to building for 1 year. At the end of that time they put the concrete paths in where the trails were in the grass. It all worked out very well.

Organizations should be put together in a somewhat similar way. It is not necessary to start up with "We need a Marketing Department" and "We need a Sales Department" and "We need a Purchasing Department" and "We need a Production Department" and "We need such and such." It depends on the work of the company. There are certain functions that must be identified because they are special and they are basically the same in every company, such as the Accounting Department, Human Resources, and so on. These are the functional operations.

The organization chart should be well displayed, with all blocks the same size and all names the same size, recognizing that it is a communication.

ORIENTATION, NEW EMPLOYEE

The day employees begin their new jobs is the day they are the most receptive to learning. It is a great time to start them on their understanding of the company. Learning goes on forever, but orientation can be done early. Employees will be impressed that the company took time to familiarize them with its operation. A spokesperson should point out that workers like to do things right the first time and that the company supports the community and should explain all the other policies of the company.

New employees should be carefully introduced to their co-workers and given a tour of the entire organization. This can't happen all in 1 day necessarily, but it should all be completed before they start to work. The orientation should not take any more than 3 days. If there is special training required, and there should be, the employees come back after they have spent a little time on their jobs. This lets them have a better idea of what is happening.

Some of the things that need to be covered in new employee orientations are purpose, policies, quality plan, security, benefits, procedures and how to look them up, internal communications, and introduction to senior management. I prefer to see the leader personally greet each new employee within the first 2 weeks of employment.

OVERDUES

Receivables which pass the acceptable period, such as 60 days, represent a financial threat to the organization. They are an indication that there is a lack of communication with the particular customer who is not paying up. They also mean that the organization must pay interest on money to replace the money that is not coming in. Most overdues happen because of a lack of concentrated effort to keep accounts from becoming overdue in the first place. The way to prevent the situation is first to determine whether the organization has a clear policy and practice of collection. Then explain the policy to the customer and explain such terms as "due within 10 days." If the policy is to offer a discount for prompt payment, do not give the discount even when payment comes in only 2 months late. It does not take customers long to know how serious a company is about collections.

There is another side to this situation. Most overdues are caused by the companies that send the bills, not by the companies that receive them. Invoice errors, and all that the phrase implies, give the customer a reason for not paying. All these situations are called *disputes*. Finding the cause of the errors and learning to prevent them is the best defense against overdues.

OVERHEAD

Expenses that go along with the business are usually lumped into one group called *overhead*. This includes everything except direct labor that goes into the service or the product of the company. It includes such expenses as executives and their secretaries, the support services, the copy machines, the company trucks that do not deliver things, the building, the lawn, the Finance Department, the furniture—just about everything.

In a production operation, overhead will usually be at least 100 percent of the direct-labor rate. Unfortunately, a lot of this just becomes accounting gibberish, but it is something that should be looked at very carefully. This is why I think looking at revenues per employee, expenses per employee, and the difference between the two is a key to good managing. Anything which shrinks that difference should not be done unless it is absolutely a matter of survival. Each entity in the company needs to pay for itself in one way or another, or at least must not be a drag.

PARKING

In regard to colleges, it is said that with the alumni, it is the football team; with the students, it is sex; and with the faculty, it is parking.

In this day and age, parking is something that cannot be ignored. One basic rule should exist: parking should be on a first-come, first-served basis, with the exception of parking for the handicapped or emergency parking. Senior executives should not have special places. This just breeds antagonism. Every company should have a parking plan that should be completely thought out.

Shuttle buses are one way of making things less uncomfortable. Disney handles one of the world's largest parking operations with very few complaints.

PAYROLL

Part of the compensation that each employee receives comes from the payroll. At the first job I had, we were paid at the end of every day in cash. It was many years before I finally got a check. Nowadays, with direct deposit, many people never see their pay and never see any real money.

The payroll is a very important part of the company's business. In any organization, it is one obligation that has to be met. It would be nice if everyone would agree to be paid on a monthly basis. Then the payroll would need to be made only once.

Because of the complexity of withholdings, taxes, and so forth, the payroll has become a routine part of the business. Senior executives very rarely pay any attention to it. I think that at least once a year all employees should be personally handed their paychecks or the stubs that represent them by their bosses.

It is said that individuals can never understand what is involved until they have "had to meet a payroll." I never believed this until our company went through its own knothole in 1982. The balancing act and the anguish and the debt necessary to meet the payroll every month during the few months we were depressed brought me an awareness that I never had before considered.

An example of zero defects in most companies is the Payroll Department. There will be very few real errors caused by that operation.

PENSIONS

Almost every company has a retirement program of some sort. The most common type today is the *defined benefit,* in which the company makes significant planned contributions. It is very rare for the employees to contribute much toward the program.

I am beginning to think that pension programs should be small and should be supplemented by things such as 401K programs, in which income can be deferred by company support of individual retirement accounts and by thrift plans. In all of these the employee gets to put in tax-free money that accumulates and grows on a tax-free basis, with the pension providing a solid base. This takes a great financial burden off the corporation.

Today the amount of money in pension funds in the United States alone is around $4 trillion. That is 4 times the annual budget of the U.S. government. Although it is nice to have all that money being invested in things, it also represents quite a drain on the corporation's cash flow. Supplemental programs would help alleviate the problem. I think employees would feel more comfortable too. If they change companies, they would get to take all the supplemental benefits with them. Without such programs, more often than not, they would either lose their pension rights entirely or receive only a small pension at age 65.

To me, a retirement program should not be quite as structured and strict as the ones with which I am familiar. People should be able to retire at the time that they wish to retire, recognizing that there will be a reduction in their benefits if they retire early. Perhaps older employees could work at less significant jobs in the company for lower salaries, thereby making room for younger people. The difference between the income they are used to and what they would get for their new jobs could be supplemented by the pension program. There is a lot of work that needs to be done in the area of retirement programs.

PEOPLE

Organizations are people in the same manner that churches are people. Many people look at a building or a church and say, "There is the organization." But obviously that is not true. If the people never come back, the church cannot do anything sitting there all by itself and the building cannot do anything sitting there all by itself.

Management reviews the status of its operation by looking at financial figures, results of projects, and so on. Whenever people subjects come up, they are always on an individual basis, such as whether a particular person is performing a job properly. Organizations are not truly people-oriented, in the sense of spending their time managing people. They spend their time managing the process, the projects, the money, and the facility.

If people are managed, developed, and led, all these other things take care of themselves. I think all senior executives and supervisors need a sign on their desks that says, "I am in the people business." Besides, people are much more interesting than buildings.

PERKS

Perquisites, as perks were once known, refers to privileges which are given to managers for the additional burdens that they bear. Usually these are things such as country club membership, a company car, first-class travel, maybe extra insurance, and inclusion of the spouse on a trip once in a while.

Over the years perks were just casually put together, but now they have become more formal. I think they make a great deal of trouble. I do believe that senior executives should get country club membership and things like that. I also believe that when off-site meetings are scheduled, spouses should be included because they are a very valuable part of the organization. Too many companies ignore them.

However, obvious perks produce an antagonism in people

who do not get them. So the key word is "obvious." In practical terms it is necessary to reward people who have a special talent, a special value to the company or organization. However, it is possible to provide other people with things that are important to them too. True perks should be selected and applied strictly by the office of the president and not by the Personnel Department.

PERMISSION

I like to say that people need permission to do things right. This sounds like a rather glib phrase, but if you think about it, it becomes very significant. Management tends to put restrictions on people in terms of setting priorities for what is important in their work, so it becomes a matter of getting it done rather than getting it right.

Management has to go to great lengths to show people that they have permission to do the job as planned, correctly and on time, with the right attitude. This is particularly true of people who are in creative operations or who feel they are in creative positions. We continually run into people who say, "Well, management does not want that to happen." Then we say, "Have the managers ever told you that?" They say, "No, the managers have not told us that, but we just know it." "How do you know?" "Well, it is just the way they act."

In this regard, it can be seen that managers have to be very careful about their body language and the other reactions that they make to show whether things are important to them. The business of giving people permission to do the job right is something that cannot be assumed by those who run things.

PERSONNEL EVALUATION

The only proper evaluation is a group evaluation in which a person's work is looked at by all the people who interface with that person. This sort of analysis will provide a true exposure of how the work is viewed.

It is up to the supervisor who leads this discussion, backed up or trained by the Human Resources people, to add personality and other aspects. Then the individual can discuss the evaluation with the supervisor without necessarily knowing who participated and can find out the results. Corrective action can be planned in terms of personal development. Also, this provides executives with the knowledge of who should be considered for a promotion or for further career planning.

Personnel evaluations should be conducted at least once a year with a follow-up regularly and should never, never, never be tied into raises. If that is done, all become suspect.

PHYSICAL, ANNUAL

Every employee should receive an annual physical. This is important not only for the obvious benefits of regular checkups but for the fact that it shows that the company cares about its employees. Senior people may be sent away to a clinic where they can spend 2 or 3 days relaxing. There is a very practical reason for this: it is often about the only way to get them to have checkups at all.

The results of the annual physical should not be given to company Personnel unless the employee particularly wants the department to have the information. Companies should also encourage the spouses to have annual physicals and, if possible, should even pay part of the cost or see whether the medical benefit plan will do that.

POLICIES

Every organization needs basic operating policies which state the company's position on many subjects. Preferably these should all be included on one page and be only a sentence or two in length. They should be included in the first part of the procedures manual, which should be given to all new employees on their first day.

Policies are established by the leader with the approval of the board of directors, and they can be changed only by the leader with the approval of the board of directors. A policy is something that cannot be waived or overcome by department heads, by executive vice presidents, or by any other individuals, no matter how important they are. In that regard, policies should be carefully thought out.

POLITICIANS

If practical, it is good for a company or an organization to have a Political Action Committee (PAC) to which people can make contributions which are then given to different political offices where people have a common interest.

For instance, it might be decided to contribute to politicians who support entrepreneurship or those who support free enterprise or those who are interested in reducing the trade deficit. This lets the PAC deal with people of whatever party on the basis of the individual effectiveness of the politician.

At no time should an organization make an individual deal with anybody in political office for anything that would benefit the company or that person. No matter how good it sounds at the moment, such action can never be properly explained because people and politicians are much too complex.

POSTERS

If an idea is to be understood and communicated, it must be put forth by every method possible. Posters explaining the need for quality, safety, or whatever, are practical to use because they're good reminders. Some of these can be hand-created, perhaps by several employees. Some can be purchased from other sources.

The most effective posters I have seen are not posters but rugs. Supplied by launderers, the rugs are used in front of doorways and say things such as, "The Fire Extinguisher Is Over There," and "We Must Do Things Right the First Time."

Posters should always be hung with dignity, not taped to a wall. They should be rotated on a planned basis, and someone should be given the responsibility for seeing that this is done

PRAYER

I believe that prayer has an important role in the life of an organization. I think that all official company meetings should be begun with a prayer that thanks the Lord for relations and communication and asks Him specifically to help achieve the goals of the organization. I think this shows a mark of respect and sets a good tone for the meeting.

I notice that all meetings begun with a prayer seem to progress better than other ones. What I have learned about prayer over the years is that prayers are answered. It is best to really think about what it is you are asking for. I believe that the Lord does take a hand in the affairs of us mortals, does so specifically, and sometimes does so quite literally.

PRINTING

Most companies have a lot of trouble with printing because printers are often unreliable. They are unreliable because they do not get the story straight as to what is to be printed. The best way to handle this is to get two printers that can handle most of your needs and then work with them to make them understand that your firm wants its jobs done exactly as agreed. Get a few of your people to understand the way printers communicate, and then hold the printers' feet to the fire. Stick right to them, and do not take anything unless it is exactly what you agreed upon in the first place.

Once everyone understands the rules and how to communicate, printing is a snap.

PROCEDURES

Procedures exist to show how policies are to be implemented. A procedure is a detailed blow-by-blow account of how a specific act is conducted by specific people. It should be developed by those who have to do the job and reviewed by those who are going to receive the work and by those who watch policies. On this basis then, management can be assured that the policy is going to be implemented and employees can be assured that the job is possible to do. All procedures should go through a Procedures Committee which represents the operating entities of the company. This has to be headed up by somebody who takes procedures seriously and, at the same time, knows how to get work done quickly and how to keep an orderly meeting and an orderly manual.

PRODUCTS LIABILITY

This subject refers to situations in which users of a company's product are injured by that product and hold the company liable for the injury. Until recently, courts were taking the position that almost anything that went wrong was the fault of the producer, not the user. However, when the manufacturer includes very clear instructions and warnings with the product, it seems to help reduce liability. The main way to avoid product safety problems, which is the proper phrase for products liability, is to be very serious about product qualification.

This means that the product should be used and improved in laboratories and in real-life trials prior to being placed on the market. Also, any kind of response from a customer that indicates a problem should be followed up very actively. Almost every significant product safety problem that wound up with a big court settlement had been raised to the supplier long before it ever went to court. At that time, if the supplier had made a proper apology and a proper change in the product and had shown some proper remorse, the big court settlement probably would not have happened.

My experience has been that it is usually the same people inside a company who produce the problems every time. These are people whose standards and integrity are shoddy when quality is compared with schedule or cost. Identifying these people early and moving them to an area where they can't do any harm is one of the best defenses against product safety problems.

PROFESSIONALS

Professionals are individuals who follow an agreed-upon set of standards for learning to do whatever it is they do and who receive accreditation for their skills. Some professionals have degrees, such as doctors, lawyers, dentists, and accountants. Most of them have state boards or state licenses. However, there are many people who pass themselves off as professionals, particularly in the area of financial management and financial planning. As far as I know, there is no accreditation in these areas.

Inside an organization, the title of professional must be considered much more broadly. It refers to people who have identifiable skills in areas such as design, inspection, quality control, and human resources. Whatever their field, they have been in it for a little while. They like to be thought of as professionals, and there's no harm in it. In fact, it makes their work much more precise.

However, professionals often tend to band together against progress. So recognize their hard work, but offer them no control.

PROFIT

All organizations need to make a profit. In volunteer or not-for-profit organizations, excess funds are not called profit. In profit-making organizations, profit can be planned by arranging the prices or arranging the expenses and by understanding all the rules and regulations of accounting. A company should make at least 6 or 7 percent after tax if it is to be thought of as a successful profit-making organization. This enables the company to give an adequate return to the shareholders and to set aside money for future development.

Profit by itself is not a really good way to measure the performance of the senior executives because if profit is the primary criterion, they can hold back on other necessary expenses in order to make profits rise. When they leave to go on to more important jobs, a great deal of maintenance and rebuilding has to be done inside the company.

PROFIT SHARING

One of the best ways of setting up an incentive for employees is to let them share in the after-tax profits. I much prefer to calculate their shares on a pretax basis, because it keeps them from being victimized by different legal—but illogical—accounting maneuvers.

Under a profit-sharing plan, a standard amount of money is put into a pool for employees. It is then distributed out of that pool on the basis of criteria such as salary, performance rating, and, in some cases, specific contributions. Formal profit-sharing programs have to be approved by the board of directors and then filed with the Securities and Exchange Commission (SEC) (in the case of a public company); they cannot be fiddled with as time goes by.

PROMOTIONS

The thing that moves people along best in companies and in their careers is that they get promoted once in a while into more responsible jobs. Unfortunately, as companies progress, many promotions are made on the basis of moving people out of jobs they are not doing very well into jobs where they can do less harm or moving people on the basis of their popularity. We all know the case where the best technician is moved up to supervisor and is a terrible supervisor, and we've lost a good technician in the process.

A promotion should not be a reward for tenure. It should be a reward for potential success in a new job. This ties into the personnel evaluation system.

When a promotion is made, everyone should know about it immediately. The individual should be told personally by someone important to her or him. The different aspects of the new position should be taken care of as quickly as possible, such as business cards, physical office location, perks that go along with the job. These all help the individual become adjusted. Also, since some people have problems adjusting, this is the time to consider counseling in the guise of development and education.

When I was moved into my first supervisory job, I received absolutely no training, and I showed it. I survived only because another assistant supervisor patiently taught me the ropes. I do not remember ever receiving any specific training for any job up the ladder during all those years. I do remember being told at least three times, "We are not really sure you are qualified for the job, but we do not have anybody else." I do not recommend that as the way to motivate a new supervisor.

PUBLIC OFFERING

There may come a time in the life of a company when it decides that it wants to go public. This means offering stock for sale to the financial world. The money received is used to expand the company and to offer a return to the originating stockholders. There really is no other way to do this, because borrowed money has to be paid back and loans debit a company. Money received from the sale of stock is tax-free and does not have to be repaid. It gives the company an opportunity to develop new products and services, make acquisitions, and do many other things that are necessary to prosper. That's the good news.

The bad news is that the preparation of an offering is a very complex thing. The leader of the company, who is used to running things on a daily basis, will find that the only thing that can be done on this matter is either to start it, which is to say, "Go ahead," or to stop it, which is to say, "Let's quit."

For a public offering, it is first necessary to find an investment banker willing to take the company public. The investment banker is usually one of the major stock houses or Wall Street houses that specialize in initial public offerings (IPOs). The banker will do an evaluation of the company, determine its worth, and get an idea of what the stock could possibly bring. All of this will be discussed with the senior executives, and then the board must decide whether to go forward.

When the "going forward" begins, lawyers from the company and from the investment brokerage house will begin the preparation of a prospectus. In doing this, they engage in a process called *due diligence.* As they create the prospectus, which describes the business and financial history of the company, they must look at every piece of paper that exists regarding the company. They must verify that the financial plan and results have been audited, which requires a great deal of teamwork.

The company people can make inputs to the prospectus on the basis of what is fact and what is not. However, the prospectus must be written entirely by the lawyers on both sides and must be agreed to by everybody. This is to ensure the investor that what is inside the prospectus is accurate. Companies have been known to fluff up their reports.

When the prospectus is complete, it is printed, filed with the Securities and Exchange Commission, and then sent out to selected brokers around the country as a "red herring." This looks like a regular prospectus, except that it has no price on it and has a red stripe down the front cover. The investment banker talks with other brokers during this time; although they have a pretty good idea what the stock price should be, they get inputs and see what they feel would hold. The idea is to pick a price which would be just a little below the real price so that when the stock goes out on the market, it can go up a little bit.

Meanwhile, the SEC is reviewing the offering. If the commission has any questions, it will write to the leader of the company for resolution. After a total of 6 weeks, the SEC usually gives approval if there are no problems; at that time, the investment banker buys all the stock that is being offered. The selling stockholders of the company, who can usually sell up to about 40 percent of the total offering, receive a check in about 10 days. In the meantime, stockbrokers are selling the stock and sending the money back to the investment banker. Within the first 30 days, the investment banker buys some more stock on the market to "prime" it; then the banker is responsible for helping the buyers and sellers get together. The stock exchange keeps it all straight.

When a company goes public, the biggest change for the company officers is that there are a lot of things they cannot do that they used to do when the company was private. For instance, they must put out a quarterly report that talks about the financial results from the previous quarter and compares them with the results of the corresponding year before. They must also send out press releases to certain people and organizations, including the SEC, whenever something significant happens inside the company, such as a promotion or a departure from the company. It is life in a fishbowl.

I examined every way possible to finance a private company while permitting some of the founders to take some money out. I could not find anything that was anywhere near satisfactory except making a public offering. It is wise to have a public relations firm with you in this so that when it comes time to make press releases and do other public things, they will be done in a professional manner.

PUBLIC RELATIONS

The image that companies project depends very much on the communications they put out to the community. This does not mean bombarding newspaper and magazine editors with information about the company. It does mean being prepared to respond and having a thought-out standard position. Public relations has to be looked at as an arm of marketing, although the two should never work for each other.

The best thing that can happen for a company or an organization is third-person credibility. This comes from customers, suppliers, and community people who respond to media requests.

Whether the company's image is important or not in the overall scheme of things, this cannot be taken for granted. A firm public relations strategy, developed with the help of a knowledgeable public relations firm, will help keep the company out of trouble. I think it is not a good idea to seek publicity, but it is sensible to respond to requests for information. A professional, well-balanced response that is not self-serving will go a long way in gaining friends for the company.

PURCHASING

Somebody has to buy everything the company or the organization uses, from pencils to printed circuit boards. It used to be that a purchasing agent would announce what was to be bought. The suppliers would then put in their bids, and the one with the lowest bid got the contract. Whatever came in came in, and the company made the best of it.

Now we have learned that suppliers have to be oriented to the needs of the company, to the purpose of the company, and to the thought that it is to the supplier's advantage to make the purchaser successful. To this end, both purchasing professionals and suppliers need to be educated. They need to understand that the supplier requires lead time to deal with what the customer wants and perhaps even to participate in the purchase requirement.

For instance, instead of sending in weekly orders for "10 pencils and 16 pieces of paper," we have a long-term arrangement. We have learned to keep an inventory of office supplies that the supplier can refurbish so that no one will ever run out. This way, the inventory will never be a burden. By the same token, we have learned that if a new component is needed for a product, the supplier can help develop it and design it in such a way that it will have the lowest cost and highest reliability.

All of this requires a new dimension in relations. The purchasing profession has not advanced as far as some of the others in relations. More time has been spent on trying to develop national contracts and other such items, all price-oriented.

"Supplier Days" should be held at least once a quarter. New suppliers should be invited to come and be oriented and to learn how to establish relations. These days should be carefully planned and not just be exhortations to do better, to cooperate, and so on. They must have a solid base and be well thought out. Material is available on quality, productivity, financing, and other topics, and it is possible to invite outside speakers. The main thing is to show the suppliers that the organization cares about them, is willing to listen to them, and is interested in long-range, long-term commitments.

PURPOSE, COMPANY

See Chapter 1.

QUALITY

Defined as conformance to requirements, "quality" is the word used when people think about getting things done right the first time. The concepts and system that cause quality to happen in any organization are described in great detail in my books *Quality Is Free* and *Quality Without Tears* (McGraw-Hill, 1979 and 1984, respectively). The main thing that needs to be understood by senior executives is that, regardless of what organizational concepts are put in place or what systems are laid in, the attitude of employees toward quality is the clear result of what they see in the attitude of senior management.

Do not confuse quality with quality control or quality assurance. They are technical disciplines in which people try to control a process through statistical and other means. They are effective as a support for a company's overall quality management process.

QUALITY CONTROL CIRCLES

This name is applied to groups of workers who gather together on a planned basis to look at the jobs they are doing and offer suggestions for improvement. It is an effective method of communication, provided it is based on a strong management-supported and -conducted system of quality improvement. Run all by themselves, quality circles are counterproductive. After a few meetings, they run out of quality ideas and begin to get into nonquality ones.

RECOGNITION

Every organization needs a planned method of recognizing the people who make contributions to the success of the organization. The program to accomplish this needs to be set up in a way that reflects the culture of the operation and also lets all the people know what is going on. For instance, everybody eligible has a 5-year pin. People are very proud of their pins and look forward to receiving them, particularly when the presentation is done in front of everybody else.

When it comes to picking someone who has done extraordinary work, it is best to rely on peer recognition. Management often is fooled into thinking that the person who is the most pleasant and who appears to be working hardest is accomplishing the most. However, many times the busy one is busy fixing things that he or she fouled up in the first place. So a peer recognition program and programs in which groups are appreciated for achieving goals are the best kinds of recognition.

RELATIVES

It is said that having relatives in the business detracts from the efficiency of the business and gives cry to charges of nepotism.

That has not been my experience. I have found that individuals who are related to the senior people in the business work twice as hard to prove they are worthy. Also, we have summer interns who are almost inevitably the children of employees. They, in turn, work extra hard in order to avoid embarrassing their parents or whoever is sponsoring them. Almost everybody in our company arrived there because they were recommended by an employee of the company. The only ones we ever had difficulty with were the ones that we got from advertising or recruitment.

RETIREMENT

There comes a time when people need to quit whatever work they are doing officially and go do something else. They can relax, travel, or do whatever they would like to do. This is necessary for a couple of reasons: First, they need to move out so that other people can move in and younger people can have a chance. Second, it gives them a chance to really enjoy their lives. Everybody should learn to look at the retired years as a second career. Many people do; they write and they draw or they start little businesses or they get involved in things.

Unfortunately, retirement is considered a negative when it should be a positive. To change this, I think that every company should set up a counseling program that starts for employees who are approaching retirement. They should begin the program at about age 55. By that time, most people have come to grips with the fact that they are not going to be the president of the company or start a brand new business or something. They begin to think about their financial planning and about the things they are going to do after they retire. We all know that it is not enough to play golf 7 days a week. Everybody needs some kind of interest.

I recommend that as people get closer to retirement, say, within 5 years, they start working a 4-day week. The next year they can turn over much of their work to other people and work on special projects and assignments. Company retirement programs, as discussed in "Pensions," should support this type of activity.

Some companies have set up advisory boards in which their key retirees are formally available to the executives and managers of the company for counseling advice. Many retirees stay on the board of directors and offer help as the years go by.

SALARIES

A salary is the compensation given to an employee in the form of an agreed-upon figure paid on a weekly or monthly basis. Usually the salaried workers are those in the administrative, professional, or managerial roles, and people known as hourly paid or weekly paid are in the manufacturing or lower-level parts of the organization.

I really think it is much better to put all employees on salary. Then they can feel more like a part of the company. There is a lot less record keeping, and it is easier to handle the payroll when it is all done in the same fashion.

The big difference between salaried workers and workers in the lower-level parts of the organization is that the latter usually receive overtime. However, this can be rearranged so that they get a certain amount of compensatory time off instead. If they do receive overtime, it can be based on something other than hourly pay, which has come to be looked at as rather demeaning.

SALES

Sales of an organization are considered the amount of money that is pledged by a customer in return for the products and services to be given. When an order is given for $1000 worth of equipment, the sales can be marked up as having been $1000. However, this does not represent revenues, which is money actually received. Companies have to differentiate between sales and revenues so that they can make sure they are talking about money actually at hand.

SCHEDULING

In any organization, a lot of things have to happen on a planned basis. One of the things that has to happen is to keep everyone informed about what is supposed to happen. For this reason, somebody and someplace have to be the repository for all that scheduling. A master schedule needs to be kept so that all the events going on in the company can be known. Usually a schedule is kept for each program as part of program management.

When people in an organization talk about never knowing what is happening or about getting surprised all the time ("Nobody knows what is going on around here"—that kind of stuff), usually what they are referring to is the lack of a common scheduling point, a place where you can go and find out what needs to be done.

SECRETARY

In the old days, a secretary was someone who answered the phone, typed letters, made appointments, and generally sat in one spot and did whatever he or she was told. Now, secretaries function more as administrators and assistants. In this regard, they are responsible for the management of the office, which may be only themselves and their bosses. It is up to the two of them to have a communication that lets this happen. This, then, lets the bosses concentrate on whatever it is they do best and the secretaries concentrate on what they do best. Between them, the office flows smoothly. All of this requires a mutual trust, based on discretion and effectiveness.

One of the problems that secretaries have had over the years is that they have limited their skills to the technical aspects: typing, filing, dictation, and so forth. While these are important, they are just tools. It is possible for someone to be a secretary to a person for several years and never really understand the business or what is going on. But there is no place a young person can learn faster about the business and how to be an executive than by becoming a secretary to an executive.

SECURITY

We think of security in terms of a guard at the gate. However, in this age a great many kinds of security exist. For instance, most organizations depend heavily on their computers. They use them for all their financial figures, mailing lists, personnel data, and just about everything that goes through the operation. The data base is a valuable piece of property. It must be protected by having copies of it put into vaults so that they cannot be stolen and by having code words so that data cannot be accessed by the wrong people. I remember a case where one young person with nothing much to do one afternoon called up the entire payroll of the company, had it printed out on his computer, and found out that everybody was making more money than he was. This caused a lot of difficulty.

Security is also necessary for in-house paperwork and for the physical premises. Documents should be classified as company confidential or personal and then should be protected and not left lying about on desks.

Security is one of the orientation items for new employee introduction. It is also something that somebody has to be responsible for. Somebody has to make certain that everything is put away and locked up at night and that individuals who ignore this precaution get reprimanded. Security, particularly in a world market, has become a very important item.

SEMINARS

Meetings planned around a speaker or program are called *seminars*. These are used to pass on information on a specific subject to a specific group of people. While the speaker and the content must be selected carefully, it should be noted that a main part of a seminar really is the environment of the meeting itself. It should be held in a place that is off-site and free from interruption. It should be carefully planned and thought out in terms of the roominess of seating arrangements, the comfortableness of the chairs, the type of media support that is available, the food, and the whole business in which the participants are going to be immersed for that day. Also, the attendees should have time to chat with each other and not be rushed in and out.

It is hard to tell in advance whether a seminar is going to be worthwhile. The only ones who can really judge are the people who will attend the seminar, not the professionals who are responsible for conducting it. All the members of an organization should go to at least one seminar a year. There, they will get some ideas about how to make their own jobs more productive.

SMOKING

No one I ever heard of thinks smoking is good for anybody, but a lot of people do not think it is too bad. Obviously this is so, because a great many people continue to do it even though there is considerable evidence that it is a destructive habit. Organizations need to provide a place where people can smoke if they choose to. However, that place does not have to be in the office. My recommendation is to have smoking lounges and to prohibit smoking at desks and in meetings. Hotels, restaurants, and other public places should separate smokers from non-smokers.

SOFTWARE

It is becoming true that "the person who rules the software, rules the world." All the computer technology we rely on so much is useless without the proper software. Software really is the instruction list that lets the electronic functions of the computer switch to the proper areas and provide the proper calculations. Computers, of course, are not smart in their own right. They are only smart in their ability to respond to the commands of the software. For many people, software is some black art that can be accomplished only with a great deal of chanting and incense burning. Actually, it is a very clear process that is good or bad, depending on the amount of time and thought put into the writing of the specification from which the software program is derived.

Software needs to be coordinated throughout any organization utilizing the same data base. There are a great many commercial software programs developed by different companies that can be utilized without creating a specific one for each specific company in each specific instance. To take advantage of this merely requires laying out the concept of the firm's data base and usage in a way that is compatible with the commercial software. While this may impose some limitations, it provides protection too. If all the software is specially designed, then the organization becomes obligated to the one group or one person who understands it. This puts everything in a very difficult position from management's standpoint. It means that managers cannot control a whole important segment of the company because they do not know what to do about it. They do not know how to understand it.

STOCK

All profit-oriented companies that are incorporated have to have stock. Of course, public companies have stock as a matter of course. Usually, the holders of these shares of ownership elect the officers of the company and vote on specific actions as requested by the Board of Directors, who, in reality, represent the stockholders.

When a new company begins, it is very important to determine how the stock is going to be distributed, who is going to have what, and what they will have to do to get it. In many entrepreneurial situations, it is necessary to give people stock in order to bring them aboard. It is not necessary that this be voting stock though. It is possible to distribute what will become the capital gains of a successful business without taking control out of the hands of the individuals who started the company.

In most cases, it is best to work out an arrangement in which the employees can participate in the ownership of the company through an ESOP or through direct outright purchases or gifts of stock. One thing that should be covered is a right of first refusal, in which the company could purchase back stock from someone who leaves. This is important because it is not always possible to determine in advance that everybody is going to be happy and loving for the entire life of the corporation.

The corporate secretary is in charge of stock, and the company attorney's office retains the absolute record of who has what and what they paid for it. When a company goes public, it has to have a transfer agent, which is usually a bank, that handles all the sales and purchases of the stock by the public and by the insiders.

STOCK OPTION

It is possible to give people options to buy stock and, at the same time, provide them with a motivating force. The option works this way: People are given certificates that say they are entitled to purchase X shares of stock at whatever the market value is at that given moment. This means that if, through their efforts and the flow of the company, the price of the stock rises, then they can purchase the stock at a significantly lower price than the market price and make a profit on it.

Usually there is a vesting time involved, which means that in order to own 100 percent of the option, employees have to have worked at the company for a certain period, usually for about 5 years. This ensures that the stock option stimulates people over a long term.

STRATEGY

Every organization needs to know where it is going and how it is going to get there. I do not believe it is possible to see much further than 1 year in advance as far as day-to-day occurrences go, but some things take a long time to build. If the strategy is to consolidate all the warehouses, this may take a couple of years because the leases need to expire, construction needs to be done, loans need to be arranged, and so forth. There are really different kinds of strategies.

The senior people of the company need to go away from everything for 2 or 3 days and, perhaps under the guiding hand of a consultant, examine the strategy of the company. They need to look at the purpose of the company. They need to look at its resources, its goals, and its customers and to examine all these things and lay them out in a nice neat order before deciding where they are going to go. It is a mistake just to sit and guess at where they want to go without realizing that getting there requires trained people, resources, and the market. Having put all this together, the group members can then determine what they would like to see happen several years from now, what they would like the company to look like, not only in terms of profitability and sales but in terms of employees, markets, and places of working. For instance, it might be desirable to have an international operation functioning in 5 years. Well, they can then backtrack from that goal and determine what building blocks will be necessary to make something happen 5 years from now.

Once the resources and goals are understood, the group can put together, piece by piece, the necessary products, people, and money to make it all happen. If it is apparent that these things are not available, then the strategy needs to be restructured. Every 6 months from then on, the group members should get together to see how things are coming and to determine whether it is necessary to revise the strategy.

Once the initial strategy is laid out, it should be given to people in the next level of operation for their comments and inputs. After all, these are the people who actually have to implement the strategy, and it is necessary to have them "buy off" on it. It is not possible to have everybody in the company go away for a strategy meeting. Some people have to be left out. However, they do not have to feel that they are left out of implementing the strategy and contributing their inputs.

Once a strategy is complete, it should be documented rather informally, and everybody who has a part in it should receive a copy. This lets them all have a common language. One thing companies miss is that having done all this, they hire a new executive and don't bother telling that person about the strategy.

SUBSCRIPTIONS

One of the big contributions to the dull life of American executives is that they read a very limited amount of material. Usually they're religious about reading the trade materials for their particular profession or industry. However, the broader, more general things slip past them. I think that all executives and developing managers should at least read *Business Week, Fortune,* and *Forbes* and news magazines such as *Time, Newsweek, The Economist,* and *The Wall Street Journal* on a daily basis. They need to read all these, not necessarily to learn how to do something, but to see what is going on, what other people think, and how other people failed.

I think it is a good investment for a company to purchase subscriptions for its executives and managers if there is no other way to get them to broaden their reading habits.

SUCCESS

Nothing comes in so many packages or is as difficult to define as success. One person's success is another person's step along the highway. Most measurements of success are oriented around business or financial gain or achievement. Some require a medal from Congress. I remember once hearing a doctor say that no one ever said on the deathbed, "I wish I had spent more time at the office."

Those who are successful, or consider themselves successful, have achieved some of the goals that they established for themselves. To this end, it is necessary to encourage people to have identifiable, measurable goals and to have the feeling of accomplishment once they reach them. At that time, they probably will set new, far more distant goals.

I think a good definition of success is listed in the sixth chapter of Micah.

SUCCESSION

Hardly anybody likes to give up power or even to share it. And, in reality, power is very difficult to share. The captain has certain overall duties. The first mate has duties. The first mate can do a lot of things, but there are some things that only the captain can do. It is not possible to have two captains. However, it is necessary for the captain to recognize that there comes a time when a replacement is necessary. For that to happen, the captain has to train, help train, help identify, or somehow or other come by someone who will take over the job and hopefully keep the ship off the rocks and headed in the same general direction as before.

It is very difficult to find a strong leader who has another strong leader as backup. This only happens when leaders recognize that there is something different they would like to do, or something additional they would like to do, and that they are willing to turn over the reins of power in order to go off and do it. Very few entrepreneurs are willing to turn over their leadership or even to train anybody along that line. They will turn away from people once they become too competent. This is why many entrepreneurial firms begin to fail once they reach a certain size. They cannot grow any further because the leader cannot reach clear across the entire organization.

The fact that many companies have lasted for years and years, through all kinds of natural and economic disasters, has shown that leadership lurks about everywhere. It is a matter of setting up a plan and following it.

SUPERVISOR

Supervising is a lost art. Most companies just take the person who is the best at doing whatever job is involved and make that person the supervisor, without any additional training. Actually, the person doing the job best probably is a technically oriented or thing-oriented person, whereas supervisors need to be people-oriented. Of course, some persons fit both categories.

Each organization, no matter how small, needs a standard orientation for supervisors to make certain that they understand all the policies of the company. This is a good time for the boss to sit down with the about-to-be supervisors and go over these one-line policies, one at a time, explaining what they mean and the reason behind them. Then, the supervisors need some outside training in personal communication, and they need to understand that they represent the management to the people, not the people to the management. By the same token, they have to be sensitive to the needs and problems of individuals.

Supervisors also need training on how to schedule and how to manage programs. The supervisor carries out the orders and instructions of the manager. This job can be thought of as the first sergeant in the Army or the chief petty officer in the Navy, where the course and target are selected and the individual units are required to perform their specific jobs in order to make this whole come together. First-line supervisors are almost always the hardest to get to change because they are very sensitive to management's desires and they want to make sure management is serious about something before they will go along with it.

SUPPLIERS

Suppliers are always thought of as being outside the company, such as vendors. However, everyone inside the organization receives material or input of some sort from other persons in the organization. So suppliers are also internal. We must make certain that the effort of communication is extended to internal suppliers to the same degree as it is to external suppliers.

A great deal more is said on this subject under "Purchasing."

TAKEOVERS

When somebody wants to take over a company it is because the person perceives that the company is not being managed to its fullest extent. Most takeovers involve offering a price for the stock of the company that is higher than the price listed on the stock exchange. The difference between these two numbers is caused by what the takeover person sees as value, which the stock market does not properly credit. Many companies, for instance, are selling stock at less than book value. This means that it would be theoretically possible to purchase the company and then break it up into pieces, sell the pieces, and wind up with more money than the company had been previously worth in stock. This happens frequently because management is so conservative in its approach and the rules of accounting are so unrealistic in terms of value that the situation is set up almost inevitably. Land and facilities, for instance, are always booked at the value that they had when they were purchased. Many companies have land that is worth millions of dollars, but because they bought it for thousands of dollars years ago, the current value is not accurately reflected on the balance sheet. However, if the land were sold, that money would come in. Companies need to reevaluate themselves—and do it properly—many times.

The best defense against a takeover is debt. A company can borrow money, buy its own shares back, and thus incur an obligation to a bank or someone else. This, then, would make the takeover agency think again because rather than buying an undervalued company, the agency would be buying a company that was heavily in debt. Debt is not a good thing to have unless you do not want to be taken over.

TARDINESS

There is no sign of disrespect that is more obvious than people who are consistently tardy. Someone who dashes into work every morning at 5 minutes past the starting time, with a different story every day, is disruptive and suspect. People are tardy only because they do not appreciate the significance of being on time. The problem should be discussed with them, and the importance of punctuality should be stressed.

Some companies have developed systems to put tardiness in its proper light. There is a positive way, in which people who have not been tardy for a year receive a special recognition, even if it's only being asked to stand up at the Family Council. And there is a negative way, in which people who are tardy more than, say, six times a year lose some benefit. The best way to eliminate tardiness is for the boss to get to work in plenty of time. If tardiness is a big problem in a company, an investigation will usually show that the senior managers are not very religious about getting to their jobs on time.

TAXES

The best advice about taxes is, "pay 'em." Working with financial consultants and an accounting firm, it is possible to interpret the tax laws and so forth to the best advantage of the organization. However, it must be remembered that taxes are the price of having a government and the price of doing business. The accrual system of accounting permits companies to set aside taxes as the year goes along. That way, they are planned for and paid, and it is not quite as disruptive.

Everyone talks about "being in the 50 percent bracket"; most companies are, and certainly a lot of senior executives fit that bill. However, I do not know of anyone who actually pays that much tax. It is used only as an argument for not doing something. Most companies in the manufacturing area pay 20 to 25 percent tax, maximum. Some of the larger ones that take advantage of depreciation and development losses don't pay any tax. Companies in the service areas wind up paying more taxes because they usually don't have all that many assets to depreciate. I think our company paid in excess of 40 percent almost every year.

TEAM

A team is a group of people selected to achieve a particular task. There is a lot of talk today about "team building" and such, and it is a very important thought, even though the techniques may not always be effective. A team is really a concept, and the purpose of the leader of a team is the same as that of the leader in a company—to pull everything together and get it all defined, to get everybody working, to overcome the personality conflicts, and to keep everybody's eye on the goal. A specific team for a specific task should also have a specific time limit on its life. It is not necessary for a team to go on forever on the same task. It is much better to have a victory party and disassemble the team and then to assemble a brand new team to pick up some necessary aspect of that particular task. I think that it takes about three meetings for a team to begin to pull itself together and about ten meetings after that for the members to get tired of each other. Team meetings should always have an agenda, and minutes should be taken at the meetings. Every task that is going to be accomplished should be assigned to a specific person or persons with a specific date for accomplishment. Teams should make periodic status reports to the senior executive responsible for them and should do it en masse. This way the senior people can determine whether the team is, in reality, cohesive in its work or whether there are conflicts that are not resolved. Above all, a team should have as its objective something measurable so that the members will know when they are done.

TELEPHONES

Everyone picks a telephone system right the second time. The problem with telephones is all the bells and whistles that are on them nowadays, particularly in the office systems. The people selecting them get so involved in all the abilities to call forward and have conference calls and such that they forget about the basic mechanics of the system, which is that it should receive calls and transmit calls.

The telephone system is usually bought for its technical capabilities. However, a team of real people who may not know much about telephone systems, but who use them all the time, should be set up to support the technical people and actually work with them on selecting a telephone system to see whether it fits in with their mode of operation.

The question then comes up as to whether it is best to buy or lease. I think that it is much better to buy, as long as service is assured. If there is any question about the service, lease the system. Then the service company will have some of the responsibility also.

TIME CHANGE

There are two main things involved with changing time painlessly. The first is attitude. It is necessary to change your watch, change your mind, change everything so that as soon as you get on the plane you are in the time zone you are going to arrive at. Think that time zone. Live that time zone. Do not keep saying to yourself, "Oh my, back home it's only seven o'clock."

The second aspect is sweets. Do not drink any alcohol at all. Lay off the ice cream and other sweets; they seem to stimulate the body at the wrong times. There is a lot that I do not understand about it, but even the slightest bit of alcohol interferes with the ability to adapt to the time change.

Upon arrival in the new zone, just go about your business at the same hours as usual. In the afternoon there will be a sinking for a couple of hours. That is a good time to sit down quietly and maybe even take a rest for an hour, but set the alarm so that sleeping does not go on too long.

There is a lot left to be understood about time changes, but a few things not readily apparent are helpful to know about. For instance, the difference between the east coast of the United States and Japan is usually 12 hours. This means that two of the meals regularly eaten are eaten at the same time in both places. Breakfast is eaten instead of dinner and dinner instead of breakfast. It is only luncheon that is eaten in the middle of the night in Japan, according to the east coast. So luncheon should be a very light meal of fruit, which is extremely easy to digest all by itself. Otherwise, the time difference in Japan of

12 hours turns out to be easier to handle than the time difference in London or Paris, which is only about 5 hours. Ninety-
nine percent of it all is attitude.

TITLES

Everyone should have a title. It is only when titles are too
descriptive and too numerous that firms get into trouble. A
company that has only one president has one happy person. A
company that has presidents of divisions and other entities, as
well as the corporate president, has a lot of happy people.

Titles are something that people outside the company can
relate to, and they make people inside the company feel better.
They also establish communication levels. A title lets the company representative deal with someone in the client or supply-
ing company who is at a level equivalent to the representative's
title in that company. Titles are not to be taken lightly.

TRAINERS

People who teach within corporations have become known as
trainers. This is really not a kind designation. What is needed in
companies to help individuals develop is an education program
which is run by educators. Training relates to skills and is asso-
ciated with teaching people to wrap solder joints or balance
balls on their noses. So referring to these people as trainers
provides them with a trainer mentality, which means that they
feel they can teach anything they can get hold of and that they
do not relate readily to concepts.

TURNAROUND

If a company gets into trouble, it usually looks to someone
outside the company, or to some person nobody has paid much
attention to inside the company, to step in and conduct a turnaround. This turnaround consists of getting hold of cash, cut-

ting back on expenses, making new deals with the lenders, perhaps issuing some stock in order to get some funds, eliminating products that don't carry their own weight, and generally taking all the hard actions that management should have taken beforehand. If it had, there would not be any need for a turnaround.

Every year, each company should sit down and pretend it is in great difficulty. The managers should ask what they would do if they had to get everything straightened out in 30 days, and then they should implement some of the ideas they come up with. It is easy to get fat in a hurry.

UNIONS

I have never had a problem with the union in my work in quality. It has always been my experience that unions were interested in getting things done the way they should be, if for no other reason than job security. Many companies and unions have a running quarrel over the years, and regardless of what they say, it all comes down to a lack of mutual respect. Company managers, on their part, tend to categorize union people as not interested in the future of the company and as only interested in the power that they can get. Managers are fond of pointing out that union people have to get elected every year. This is the very reason that union executives need more understanding from company management. They need to be able to show that they are communicating and are having success. Otherwise, they have to do dramatic things.

Union executives could be more amenable to communications and to reaching out. They could do a little more studying in regard to what is involved in running a company and, also, how to tell management how the people feel.

In the world market today, there is no room for quarrels.

VACATION

Very few business people know how to take a proper vacation. They try to do it in dribs and drabs, taking a weekend here and a few days there. When they do go away for a week or so, they tend to call in every day and to try to run the office from wherever they happen to be. This is very disturbing for the people they are sharing the vacation with, it is disturbing for the people in the office, and it offers no rest for the vacationer. Anyone smart enough to run a business or any other organization should be smart enough to know that it takes about 10 days before a vacation begins to take effect. Therefore, vacations of at least 2 weeks should be taken, preferably 3 weeks. (Employees should not be allowed to break their vacations up into little bits either.) Vacations should be in a place that offers a completely different view of the world than the day-to-day experience, and they should not be scheduled down to each little bit of time.

The vacationer should offer to purchase a dinner for everyone in the office should a "call-in" be made. A single phone call to see how things are going would be enough to trigger that payoff. By the same token, people in the office should learn how to run things when the boss is not there.

With proper planning, a family can see a great deal on regular vacations. Children do grow up; they become parents and vacationers themselves, and they need to learn good habits. I have found it to be valuable to have one place that is used regularly for vacation. This gives everyone a chance to get to know the area and the people and actually establish a sort of second home.

VACCINATION

Preventive medicine has come a long way since the days when the plague and smallpox epidemics used to wipe out half a country in a month. Now we have learned that the body can be innoculated against certain diseases and can, in fact, avoid the danger of ever catching them.

It is the same with a business. There are certain actions which can be taken to keep the business from ever having a serious disease. In *Quality Without Tears*, I described a vaccine that would protect a company from ever having problems with quality. Similar things can be thought out for general management, finance, and other areas. The main thing is to recognize that the diseases of business do not suddenly appear overnight. They have been festering and growing unrecognized.

VARIANCE

This used to be a manufacturing term aimed at how much defective material would have to be produced in order to get the right amount of deliverable material. In shops, workers would be issued 110 pieces with the expectation that they would wind up with 100 usable parts.

Variance has also become a financial term, having to do with difference in the plan. I do not care for any kind of planned variance.

VALUE

Did you receive what you paid for? Did you get your money's worth? That is what value is all about. In running a business or any other organization, it is necessary to give the customers the feeling that they are getting something for their efforts or their funds. Value is not some mysterious vague thing that you know or don't know when you see it. Value is real, and it can be calculated in financial terms.

Interviewing customers concerning what they wanted from their purchases or what they thought of the service they received from you will help to identify these values.

YELLING

Ladies and gentlemen do not yell at each other.

YOUTH

Youth is a situation that is overcome by having lived a while. It is also a time when one can learn a complete foreign language in a summer and lift sofas to move them to the other side of the room. I recommend peppering any organization with youth, just on the general idea that young people will contribute through their earnestness.

Each young person who is brought aboard should be brought in with the thought that someday that person could work her or his way up to be leader. My experience in working for several companies that hired me when I was young was that in their opinions I was never going to get old. Time and again I would see people with less understanding of what should be done put over me because they were older and had been around for a long time. It was not until I went to the Martin-Marietta Corporation in 1957 that I found that age was not the significant criterion in selecting people to run things.

11

Following Through

The product is the organization, and the organization is the product.

People trust brand-name products because of the reputation of the company that produces them. People purchase goods in hotel shops when they go to strange places because they feel the hotel somehow regulates the items.

People give to some charities with pleasure; they are not too sure about some others. Most colleges are well thought of; some do not give a clear image.

When we are running something, we have to get it firmly fixed in our minds that our customers and the public do not look at us solely through the product we deliver, whether it be in a box or an envelope. A bank is a bank, and from a business viewpoint one can do little that the other cannot.

The complete organization is on view at all times. Customers look at the furniture, the politeness of the employees, the housekeeping, the sturdiness of the letter paper, the driving habits of company vehicles, the tone of the advertisements—everything counts.

We can never let up on making certain that every little detail is in place—and stays there. It is vital that employees have the ability to communicate to decision makers without fuss. They are the first line of awareness that the ramparts are beginning to deteriorate a little.

But most of all, the ones in charge have to keep on their toes. They have to be aware and follow through. They have to keep their minds on the key phrase, which sounds a little strange at first but makes sense as you absorb it: *The product is the organization.*

Helping decision makers recognize that everything they do affects everything that goes on in the organization requires establishing a constant awareness. Some will recognize the significance of it all and some won't.

It is easy to create lists of things for others to do. No aspect of a work situation is exempt from having that happen. People who run things are overwhelmed by information that is both helpful and not helpful. Searching for the secret understanding that everyone else knew but me, I have read everything that has come along over the years.

Most of what is known is interesting and useful but makes little difference except as part of a total. Being able to conduct an interview skillfully, for instance, contributes to a fuller executive life but does not guarantee success in itself. There are interviewees who are skillful also.

The business of causing things to run is the broadest of fields and cannot be completely defined and prescribed. It has to be conducted in a natural manner. The good news is that naturalness can be brought out once individuals understand themselves in light of the necessary information.

What appears as natural in a person is usually the result of a prepared and thought-out effort. A beautifully "built-in" golf swing is the result of hours of muscle memory training. The accomplished speaker may have spoken for days to the roaring surf with a mouth full of pebbles. "Naturalness" can be learned.

The thoughts that were mentioned earlier on conviction, commitment, and conversion apply here very clearly. Keeping tabs on all the strings involved in running an organization and making the proper moves at the proper times are within the grasp of anyone who cares to work at it. Life is much more rewarding when we are able to make things happen our own way.

Every coach, regardless of the sport, repeats the same phrase to the athletes: "Follow through."

It is possible to determine whether someone is a good athlete by just watching the person throw a ball. He or she begins the throw with a body-weight shift, putting most of the weight on the foot that is on the same side of the body as the throwing arm.

The throwing arm and hand sweep back, and the weight begins its move to the other foot, just ahead of the arm's arc. The ball is released as the "whip" of the body's movement accelerates the arm. The hand aims the ball at the target and releases the grip at precisely the correct moment to achieve the maximum velocity.

After the ball is on its way, the body keeps moving and completes the throw with the hand on its way to the area of the knee or ankle. The ball is already a long way off when the body is finishing the throw.

A tennis player, a swimmer, a golfer, or anyone involved in a physical sport has to follow through because that is the only way the necessary acts can be accomplished completely. People who have learned to do it this way follow through in every physical act they do. They walk that way, they gesture that way, they even fall gracefully.

Many of us have worked for individuals who seemed to have secret vision. Show them a complex report that a staff of eight spent 6 weeks assembling, and they will find the only erroneous calculation in it. Or they will ask the one question that no one thought to ask; or they will wonder why we are doing it at all—and no one has a good answer.

How do these people know these things? How do they sense them? Why do they look at reports differently than those who prepare them? When they ask, "What did Smedley say?" we all realize that we never gave Smedley a thought. And, of course, she is a vital part of making the project a success. What do they have that we don't have?

Nothing, actually. We all have the same things but we use them differently, and some do not use them at all. The ability to comprehend, analyze, and generate thought comes from accepting the responsibility for something and having learned how to follow through. It is necessary to be last, or at least to think that way.

The person responsible for ordering dinner for a meeting is going to look at the menu carefully. Each option will be thought about and accepted or rejected with the realization that the decision will have to stand scrutiny. People who order dinner are the last in the chain. Whatever they select is what is going to happen. To maintain the respect of those involved, the decisions made must be able to stand examination. They must be prudent.

In short, the task is taken seriously. The success or failure of past dinners is examined; the likes and dislikes of those involved are remembered; the traditions and holidays of different religious or national groups are considered; the social trends toward light or heavy meals are taken into account.

The capability of the chef, the kitchen, the serving staff—all of these have to be given consideration. After a complete evaluation of the job, a decision is made. Recognizing the time limitations, and the fact that this is not the last meal that will ever be served, the responsible person does all this in a minimum amount of time and does it well. It doesn't take forever because of the concentration applied. It is done naturally.

Naturalness has to do with putting all the knowledge, experience, and planning of a person into a "searchlight" that concentrates on the project. A short burst of energy is applied, and everything that needs to be thought about is thought about. Staff members are amazed at the completeness of the action because they are used to doing things over several times in order to get results.

"Naturals" know that they are probably going to get only one shot at a problem, and they would not want more than one anyway.

What all this leads to is that managers should be so converted that they do not need to remind themselves that the head must be held still, the arm straight, the sweep steady, and so forth. As we all know, the swing is over by the time the complete memory system is recalled.

Early in the book I talked about the basics of an organization, concentrating on things such as purpose and charter. These are the foundation of being a natural and doing follow-through as a normal part of doing anything.

The purpose and the charter, as well as other policy decisions, have to be remembered in total and considered as part of every decision. This is the "secret" of the all-encompassing mind.

Our policy is to treat all employees alike. Everyone has the same medical benefit program, the same retirement formula, and the same everything. Salaries vary depending on experience, education, and such, but all come from the same base. We have made this policy because we know that people work better when they feel appreciated and when they know that others are not being treated in a special way.

Suppose we buy a new building and in the basement of that building are a dozen parking spaces. The facilities manager wants to know who should be assigned to those spaces.

"Nobody," should be the answer. "We can use them for parking company vehicles, for emergencies such as someone in a wheelchair, and for storage. But no individuals, including me, will use them."

There are a dozen very logical reasons for painting names on parking spots. But unless there is a spot for everyone, such a policy causes a constant festering sore that disrupts the organization. This one little act of privilege would send out a message that causes people to revise completely their opinion of the organization—negatively.

If our operation is in charge of the symphony and someone comes along with an offer to add a retail pet shop to our responsibilities, we need to remember the charter and decline with thanks. We should deal with businesses we know something about.

Notice that the corporations which combined many varied companies in one conglomerate are now disentangling those companies. It is becoming apparent that the synergy which one business can bring to another just doesn't happen. Being in the hotel business and owning a car-rental firm does not guarantee that each will make more money.

The problems come from the different ways the managers of those two entities think. True, both deal with the traveling public, and true, both have short-term relationships, but there the matter ends.

The car rental company sees the customer only once, or perhaps twice—when the person rents the car and when the person turns it in. The company doesn't have to attend to the varied wants of that person over the several days they are doing business together. The hotel, on the other hand, has to serve as a home to the customer, clean up after the person just as mom did, and provide entertainment into the bargain.

The executives making decisions in the two companies have entirely different views of the customer. To switch them around and expect them to be effective, or to expect their superiors to be flexible enough to understand what each is talking about, is a little much.

Car rental companies make their money when they sell the cars on the used-car market. In the meantime, they hope that the operating income will add a little to the pot. Hotels make their money on cash flow and perhaps a little depreciation.

The same disorientation is true in manufacturing. Companies think that they can add products to the lines and use the same salespeople to sell them.

"After all, they are making a call anyway" is the thought.

So the veteran salesperson who knows everything that could ever be known about fasteners is now in the position of trying to peddle electronics. What the boss hasn't recognized is that a different person buys electronics in the customer's shop and the salesperson has zero relations with that person. Also, there is a completely new language involved.

Running things requires a complete understanding of what the organization is all about and where it plans to go. It has to be clear in the mind of the runner. This does not mean a 6-pound plan of execution; it does not even mean a clear view of the horizon. But it does mean a comprehension of what needs to be accomplished.

Entrepreneurs succeed when they just can't sleep until everyone has one of their products or until their company is recognized as the best in its field. They do whatever is necessary to make that happen, keeping a firm eye on the target and a firm hand on the tiller. They never forget what task they are about.

The footprints that are left from successful activities have a lasting power proportionate to the understanding by the people who built and ran the companies: that the organization is the product.

Guidelines for Browsers

Leadership is a fascinating subject; all of human history revolves around it.   v

Leadership is a practical tool of everyday life. Each of us leads something, even if it is only taking a reluctant animal for a walk each evening.   v

One of the requirements for being a successful leader is making time to sit and read and just learn more about the task.   v

I have always considered myself a closet grasshopper who recognizes that ants survive and prosper while grasshoppers start over again each year. Being practical, I have donned ants' clothes.   vi

The purpose of organizations is to help people have lives.   1

Everything about us came from some organization.   2

The useful organization can be constructed and managed in an atmosphere of joy and satisfaction.   3

What "professional" means in this company: ADEPT—Accurate, Discreet, Enthusiastic, Productive, and Thrifty.   4

People *do* need a reason for doing.   16

They never really put themselves into the job until they understand what their personal roles are in making the project happen.   16

All individuals want to make a contribution.   16

Every year I find out something that others have known for years.   16

If employees are being asked to "do it right the first time," then they are entitled to know what "it" is.   16

The first thing to do is to work out the details for accomplishment and decide who is going to do each task.   17

Requirements are communications.   17

Requirements must be taken seriously or they don't matter.   17

The leader has no more important concern than helping all the people involved reach the conclusion that they are important to the undertaking and it is important to their world.   17

Dedication cannot be considered a given. It has to be arranged, nurtured, pruned, and cultured.   17

Some folks work for money alone, but they are loyal only to money.   17

Everyone I ever knew who was dedicated to making a lot of dough never did.   17

People work for fulfillment, appreciation, and companionship   18

Being phony will never help dedication emerge.   18

Volunteer organizations have the advantage that very few people join without being interested in the work.   18

New employees or volunteers should be greeted as though they were guests and immediately shown a film or slide show about the history of the organization.   18

It is not advisable to paint a picture of competence and affluence during the orientation if that is not the real world.   19

Most leadership is negative in that it is directed at not failing. Not failing is not the same as succeeding.   19

Organizations have an attitude that is generated by the thought leaders.   19

All employees want to be proud of everything they are connected with and, if given the slightest opportunity, will make it something of which to be proud.   20

We now know that people really prefer a consistent standard, the same one all the time.   21

Each operation has to have a standard that cannot be misunderstood.   21

To convince everyone that they are serious, managers have to continually witness and teach.   21

The future executive can go all the way through undergraduate business school and graduate business school without receiving a course on how to help the employee.   23

The role of the senior manager is to witness.   23

Belonging to something is what people center on throughout their lives.   28

I have never met an executive who did not claim to be people-oriented.   28

The framework of an organization is really its identity.   29

We tend to take existence for granted.   29

The pitch does not exist until the umpire says it exists.   29

Most companies expect that their employees will be fully operational at the time they join.   29

The Navy and the Boy Scouts know better.   29

Management on a daily basis is made up of finding solutions for problems.   32

If the people do not know what is expected of them, the leader cannot plan on any specific occurrence.   35

Systems are the communications center of the operation. No one can do everything by himself or herself.   35

Unfortunately, most of the monitoring or controlling we do is aimed at the final product.   35

We need to be more concerned with systems integrity.   36

One inexhaustible subject for managers is communication. Somehow it never happens completely.   36

Transmission, of course, refers to the logical communication activities conducted by business people.   36

Reception refers to the listening part.   36

Meetings do not need to be punishment.   37

The same group of people who could not get enough of each other at the company picnic are bored out of their skulls at the monthly status review.   37

Very few people write with enough clarity to be understood by the willing "listener," let alone the rest of us, who merely scan what should be digested.   37

Somehow or other, each of us is expected to carve a personal way through his or her career.   37

The business world divides itself into professional and administrative areas.   38

People need reviews and consultations that let them discover their abilities and talents.   38

People must know how to bridge the gap between where they are now and where they want to go.   38

Nothing is more important for the leader than making certain that people who deserve appreciation receive it.   38

Appreciation should be part of the daily character of life.   39

Lack of appreciation is particularly evident in regard to workers in the lower levels of the organization.   39

A leader has to be a reflection of the soul of the organization.   40

One other aspect seems so obvious that I often have difficulty in getting senior executives to take it seriously. This is giving people permission to do their jobs correctly.   40

Permission to do things correctly results in getting line-stopping problems identified, corrected, and eliminated.   41

Gaining permission to do things right can be a lifelong frustration unless the leader thinks it is important too.   41

Some managers just can't let go, particularly those who become leaders. Many develop a terminal case of "big shot."   48

The leader must be a walking, talking, visible example of what the ethics of the business are to be. Policies are useful, but example is all.   49

Becoming locked into a plan is lazy management.   59

In managing change, figuring out what needs to be done is not the problem.   60

The history of wars shows that the general who was able to determine the need for change and execute it rapidly was the one who got his own way.   60

Determining the need for change, executing the change, and monitoring the success of the execution all require some formal communication system.   60

We have to be able to count on one another.   61

In order to manage a process properly, the executive needs to know what is happening.   61

Economists use statistics in great depth and complexity to put together the basic data for their analyses. But the answers they come up with are not necessarily what turns out to be true.   62

Time is life. We are allocated only so much of it; each moment is precious.   65

Meetings are our friends. Properly arranged and conducted, meetings will add years of discretionary time to life.   66

We eat for nourishment and energy. But is is possible to eat a great deal and still not be nourished properly.   66

Why are there useless, dull, mind-boggling meetings?   66

Just making up an agenda provides confidence that the meeting will be useful.   66

Visual aids can put the audience to sleep.   66

Every well-run organization should have a committee for finance and one for operations, at least.   67

Most organizations get into trouble financially because they do not know where their money is going before it goes.   67

Executive time has to be looked at as something that is assigned, not just consumed.   67

A little order never hurt anything.   67

The big users of office time are mail and telephones. The common characteristic is that neither is controlled by the recipient.   68

It is not always easy to appear as if everything is great when real problems are sitting on the leader's shoulders.   105

Employees can spot genuine interest or the lack of it from 50 yards away.   105

Sitting in the headquarters office reading reports was delusion incorporated.   105

Touring can be learned.   105

If forest managers could converse directly with the flora and fauna, they would make fewer mistakes.   105

The company changes because the "spirit" changes. People start working again.   106

When a management team offers hope and positive leadership, the people start making things move again.   106

Keeping the company from going to sleep, keeping the management team challenged and filled with dreams, offering the customers new and improved products, and creating an environment in which people enjoy hard work—this is what makes a company continually successful.   106

Apparently there is a requirement that people are permitted, perhaps expected, to produce a little pain along with their product.   125

If we really want to make a task happen, then we are willing to overlook the contra tendencies and practices of the individuals involved. 126

Anything that tastes good is bound to be bad for us.   126

I have never understood why people who are supposed to be smart have to be rude or unfeeling in their relations with others.   126

People go through life without recognizing that what they put forth as a smile, others may read as a snarl.   126

How do you know whether someone is capable of doing something? 133

There are individuals who became billionaires after being rejected by the ones who knew them best.   134

"Ability" means having the talent and energy to perform.   134

The management that tolerates people who do not show up for work sows the worst kind of seeds.   134

Those who love their work appear every day—anyway.   135

Accounting rules are not based on logic, and for the most part, the results of their application cannot be used for managing unless translated.   135

Much of the lore of advertising is aimed at the clever phrase that get° people's attention. However, the most useful advertising for the majority of companies is the routine type.   137

The best advertising is third-person credibility.   137

When I was working in the international scene, it sometimes seemed to me that half the people I knew were "functioning alcoholics," and several weren't functioning.   137

Fiction is built around people who draw incorrect conclusions from aɪ analysis of the data presented to them.   138

Running a business is like managing a flowing river.   138

The succcessful executive combines a knowledge of the past with measurements of the present to develop a strategy of accomplishment for the future.   138

The most desired of all responses is appreciation.   138

The "assistant to" is someone who is in training to become a professional.   139

I really believe that bacteria and such don't make us sick until the way we look at things depresses the body's immune system and lets the "bugs" operate.   140

People deal with life according to the way they view it, and that view reflects their attitudes.   140

Negative people can make positive people sick, and vice versa.   140

People never become so cynical that they stop thinking their birthday is a very special time.   140

A great deal of trouble can be averted by following the advice of directors who are not personally involved.   141

It is not a good idea to give people bonuses.   141

Debt is not a friend.   141

A budget is a communication system that was originally designed as an agreement between those who were going to spend the money and those who were going to provide it.   141

To most individuals, budgets are a way of tracking overspending.
142

Just as typewriters have not made letters clearer or shorter, computers have not made data less muddled.   145

Not every organization can contain within itself all the skills necessary to run a complex business.   146

There is no such thing as a standard contract.   146

Most problems have their origins in incomplete requirements or in incomplete understanding of those requirements somewhere up the line.   147

Companies need a formal system of corrective action that they can teach and repeat.   147

I don't know of any time in life when a person can't use counseling.
148

Creativity is the ability to bring something into existence that wasn't there before.   148

To create something is one thing; to communicate what has been created to others so that they can utilize it is quite another.   148

A creative idea is not in place until it can be accomplished in detail by untrained people.   148

Culture really is refinement.   148

Each organization has its own culture, which is developed very much by the values that are put forth by senior management.   148

Inside any organization, every person has a customer.   149

Every office, every organization, every factory, and every other entity needs to be decorated.   149

There is no more urgent task than helping people to be more competent.   149

Project management has to be set up to create a product that will fulfill the requirements.   150

There is no company that can continue having the same product year after year without change.   150

It is not necessary to have bullwhips and hobnail boots to have discipline.   150

The business of not treating someone differently because of age, sex, color, or whatever, is very difficult.   151

Discretion requires that people dress in accordance with the culture they live in.   151

Abuse of other forms of drugs besides alcohol is becoming more prevalent nowadays.   151

Employees have a better chance to develop the education habit if companies help pay for any course, including basket weaving, that people want to take.   152

The single most repetitive cause of failure in executive ranks, or failure of a corporation, is management ego.   152

Ego and self-confidence are at opposite ends of the scale.   153

People who are willing to take risks with their own personal resources and time in order to accomplish ideas or objectives that they hold very dear are true entrepreneurs.   153

Pseudo entrepreneurs spend all their time trying to raise money, making certain that very little of it is their own.   153

When the founder will not let anyone else really run anything, the company begins to strangle because its growth is limited.   153

The difference between a successful and an unsuccessful executive lies in the ability to communicate. Very few executives can make a good speech.   154

I can make out an expense report 6 months in advance and get it all right.   154

Management, particularly American management, is obsessed with fads.   154

Improvements in management capability come from learning through failing.   155

Never form a company with field service as a start-up operation. 156

More companies go down the chute because of improper control of the money they had than because of lack of money.   156

The status of finances should be made known to much lower levels within the company than it usually is. One of the reasons people spend money without thinking about it is that they don't think it relates to them.   157

The act of terminating somebody from a company involves more than severing the relationship between an individual and a company. 157

While checks and other items are being processed through banks, credit card companies, and other financial institutions, that money is not available to its owner.   157

Not everyone who starts up a company is a founder.   158

Freight is the commodity of transportation.   158

No executive should receive gifts from anybody in the company or from its suppliers.   159

Studies always show that the biggest source of information inside any company is the grapevine.   159

Gossip is mischievous at best.   159

The main thing to know about graphics is that they are a lot more complicated and take a lot more time than is generally thought. 160

The company that does not grow each year in revenue and profit is headed for trouble.   160

Just taking care, or planning well, does not seem to cause growth. 160

All individuals have to be concerned with expanding their knowledge and information bases in learning how to deal with the world.   160

Nothing will happen unless individuals have something they want to accomplish and go for it.   161

The leader should have at least a 2-minute interview with everybody the operation is seriously considering hiring, if only to see that the applicant's personality will fit.   161

Human Resources departments often state that the majority of complaints they usually hear are about the way their companies treat people.   162

The big difference between for-profit and not-for-profit organizations is that for-profit organizations have to take the revenue code into consideration on almost every business decision they make. 162

We have to learn to think of everything in terms of the world environment and not just the local jurisdiction.   162

The big problem with interviews is that they are usually one-shot deals.   163

Service companies do not think of themselves as having inventory and paying interest on the holding costs.   163

The business of managing inventory has changed to the business of eliminating inventory.   164

The majority of companies inside Japan are not very well managed and are not all that successful.   164

Job descriptions should not be incredibly formal; they should just be complete.   165

It is possible to take many jobs and divide them into halves.   165

"Kanban" is a Japanese phrase for zero inventory.   165

Massive layoffs of, say, 20 percent of the work force can set a company back 20 years. Think about that when hiring people.   166

Never sign a lease until your lawyer has read it.   166

The most important part of any lecture is the audience, not the lecturer or the material.   167

My personal recommendation is never lend money to anybody, particularly relatives. If the desire to help them out is overwhelming, then just give it to them.   167

Most business letters are terrible.   167

Organizations should have a place or places set aside where employees can go to sit down and relax for a few minutes.   167

People who are going to run something need a much broader understanding of the world than they can get from specialized magazines.   168

I got one of my best ideas from the back of a breakfast cereal carton.   168

To get things done, it is necessary to have a system.   168

The key to management style is the relations of the senior executives to the people they are supervising.   169

My feeling is that people are born either executives or managers and that it is possible to tell which they are by the time they are 3 years old.   169

If an organization is to have unity and do things in a routine way, it needs a manual of procedures, policies, and basic information for reference. 169

Procedures should be prepared by the people who are doing the jobs. 170

Margin is the difference between the cost of output plus cost of sales and the actual price the customer pays. 170

Marketing is what we all do with our personal careers. 170

All of us, as well as our businesses, need to think out how we wish to be presented to the world. 171

The effort that is put forth to earn an MBA is worth recognizing. 171

Measurements have to have integrity. 172

Organizations cannot hide from the media, and when they solicit the media, they get the opportunity to make big mistakes. 172

One of the myths of management is that meetings are a gigantic waste of time. 173

Only poorly managed meetings are not useful. 174

In fact, everybody is a minority in some way. 174

There is no excuse for making some people feel that they are different. 174

If MIS reports to someone at the very top of the organization, they develop an entire world of their own. 175

Money is a concept, not a reality. 175

When we talk about money, we should really be concerned about the use of money and its importance as a source of jobs and power. 176

Motels have gotten a bad name over the years because they are thought to be rather casual about their admittance policies, not necessarily very efficient, and not always very comfortable, quiet, or private. All of that is true. 176

Executives would like to have a way of getting their people charged up to do good work with no effort on their part. 176

"Pride in work" is the result of "pride in employee." 176

I have noticed that crisis brings out the best in people, while success brings out the worst.   176

There are a lot of myths in management. When myths are repeated often enough, people begin to think that they are real.   176

It is not necessary to be a genius to know that if one borrows money at 20 percent and then works to make a 10 percent return, the effort is going to sink slowly into the sea.   177

People sometimes forget that armies are built around medals of recognition.   177

Many organizations provide cramped office conditions for their employees because they think they are saving money and improving efficiency by having everybody closer together.   177

In most productive offices I have seen, there is plenty of room to walk around and plenty of room for people to be alone if they with to be. 178

Someone should be put in charge of office supplies.   178

Some organizations pride themselves on not having an organizational chart. All this does is produce confusion.   179

The day employees begin their new jobs is the day they are the most receptive to learning.   179

Receivables which pass the acceptable period, such as 60 days, represent a financial threat to the organization.   180

Most overdues are caused by the companies that send the bills, not by the companies that receive them.   181

Expenses that go along with the business are usually lumped into one group called *overhead.*   181

Each entity in the company needs to pay for itself in one way or another, or at least must not be a drag.   181

In regard to colleges, it is said that with the alumni, it is the football team; with the students, it is sex; and with the faculty, it is parking. 181

Part of the compensation that each employee receives comes from the payroll.   182

An example of zero defects in most companies is the Payroll Department. There will be very few real errors caused by that operation. 182

People should be able to retire at the time that they wish to retire, recognizing that there will be a reduction in their benefits if they retire early.   183

Organizations are people in the same manner that churches are people.   184

If people are managed, developed, and led, all these other things take care of themselves.   184

Over the years perks were just casually put together, but now they have become more formal. I think they make a great deal of trouble.   184

People need permission to do things right.   185

The only proper evaluation is a group evaluation in which a person's work is looked at by all the people who interface with that person. 185

Personnel evaluations should be conducted at least once a year with a follow-up regularly and should never, never, never be tied into raises.   186

Every employee should receive an annual physical.   186

Every organization needs basic operating policies which state the company's position on many subjects.   186

A policy is something that cannot be waived or overcome by department heads, by executive vice presidents, or by any other individuals, no matter how important they are.   187

At no time should an organization make an individual deal with anybody in political office for anything that would benefit the company or that person.   187

If an idea is to be understood and communicated, it must be put forth by every method possible.   187

I believe that prayer has an important role in the life of an organization.   188

Most companies have a lot of trouble with printing because printers are often unreliable. They are unreliable because they do not get the story straight as to what is to be printed.   188

A procedure is a detailed blow-by-blow account of how a specific act is conducted by specific people.   189

The main way to avoid product safety problems, which is the proper phrase for products liability, is to be very serious about product qualification. 189

My experience has been that it is usually the same people inside a company who produce the problems every time. 190

Professionals often tend to band together against progress. So recognize their hard work, but offer them no control. 190

All organizations need to make a profit. 190

One of the best ways of setting up an incentive for employees is to let them share in the after-tax profits. 191

The thing that moves people along best in companies and in their careers is that they get promoted once in a while into more responsible jobs. 191

For a public offering, it is first necessary to find an investment banker willing to take the company public. 193

When a company goes public, the biggest change for the company officers is that there are a lot of things they can't do that they used to do when the company was private. 194

The image that companies project depends very much on the communications they put out to the community. 194

Public relations has to be looked at as an arm of marketing, although the two should never work for each other. 194

Suppliers have to be oriented to the needs of the company, to the purpose of the company, and to the thought that it is to the supplier's advantage to make the purchaser successful. 195

The attitude of employees toward quality is the clear result of what they see in the attitude of senior management. 196

Every organization needs a planned method of recognizing the people who make contributions to the success of that organization. 197

I have found that individuals who are related to the senior people in the business work twice as hard to prove they are worthy. 198

There comes a time when people need to quit whatever work they are doing officially and go do something else. 198

I really think it is much better to put all employees on salary. Then they can feel more like a part of the company. 199

Companies have to differentiate between sales and revenues so that they can make sure they are talking about money actually at hand. 199

One of the things that has to happen is to keep everyone informed about what is supposed to happen.   200

It is possible for someone to be a secretary to a person for several years and never really understand the business or what is going on. 200

We think of security in terms of a guard at the gate.   201

It is hard to tell in advance whether a seminar is going to be worthwhile or not.   202

No one I ever heard of thinks smoking is good for anybody, but a lot of people don't think it is too bad.   202

"The person who rules the software, rules the world."   202

For many people, software is some black art that can be accomplished only with a great deal of chanting and incense burning.   202

When a new company begins, it is very important to determine how the stock is going to be distributed, who is going to have what, and what they will have to do to get it.   203

When a company goes public, it has to have a transfer agent, which is usually a bank, that handles all the sales and purchases of the stock by the public and by the insiders.   204

It is possible to give people options to buy stock and, at the same time, provide them with a motivating force.   204

Every organization needs to know where it is going and how it is going to get there.   204

The senior people of the company need to go away from everything for 2 or 3 days and, perhaps under the guiding hand of a consultant, examine the strategy of the company.   205

Once a strategy is complete, it should be documented rather informally, and everybody who has a part in it should receive a copy. 205

One of the big contributions to the dull life of American executives is that they read a very limited amount of material.   206

One person's success is another person's step along the highway. 206

A good definition of success is listed in the sixth chapter of Micah. 206

Hardly anybody likes to give up power or even to share it. And, in reality, power is very difficult to share.   207

Supervising is a lost art.   207

First-line supervisors are almost always the hardest to get to change because they are very sensitive to management's desires and they want to make sure management is serious about something before they will go along with it.   208

We must make certain that the effort of communication is extended to internal suppliers to the same degree as it is to external suppliers. 208

Companies need to reevaluate themselves—and do it properly— many times.   209

The best defense against a takeover is debt.   209

Debt is not a good thing to have unless you don't want to be taken over.   209

There is no sign of disrespect that is more obvious than people who are consistently tardy.   209

The best way to eliminate tardiness is for the boss to get to work in plenty of time.   210

The best advice about taxes is, "pay 'em."   210

A specific team for a specific task should also have a specific time limit on its life.   211

Everyone picks a telephone system right the second time.   211

There are two main things involved with changing time painlessly. The first is attitude.   212

Everyone should have a title. It is only when titles are too descriptive and too numerous that firms get into trouble.   213

Titles are something that people outside the company can relate to, and they make people inside the company feel better.   213

What is needed in companies to help individuals develop is an education program which is run by educators.   213

Every year, each company should sit down and pretend it is in great difficulty. The managers should ask what they would do if they had to get everything all straightened out in 30 days, and then they should implement some of the ideas they come up with.   214

Many companies and unions have a running quarrel over the years, and regardless of what they say, it all comes down to a lack of mutual respect.   214

The product is the organization, and the organization is the product.   219

Index

ABOUT THE AUTHOR

Philip B. Crosby is chairman of PCA, Inc., the quality management consulting firm that contains the Quality College. Begun in Winter Park, Florida, in 1979, Philip Crosby Associates, Inc., now operates internationally and is a publicly listed corporation.

Of his thirty-three years in management, Crosby spent fourteen as corporate vice president of International Telephone & Telegraph. He is the author of *Quality Is Free*, *The Art of Getting Your Own Sweet Way*, and *Quality Without Tears*.

He divides his time between Winter Park, Florida, and Savannah, Georgia.